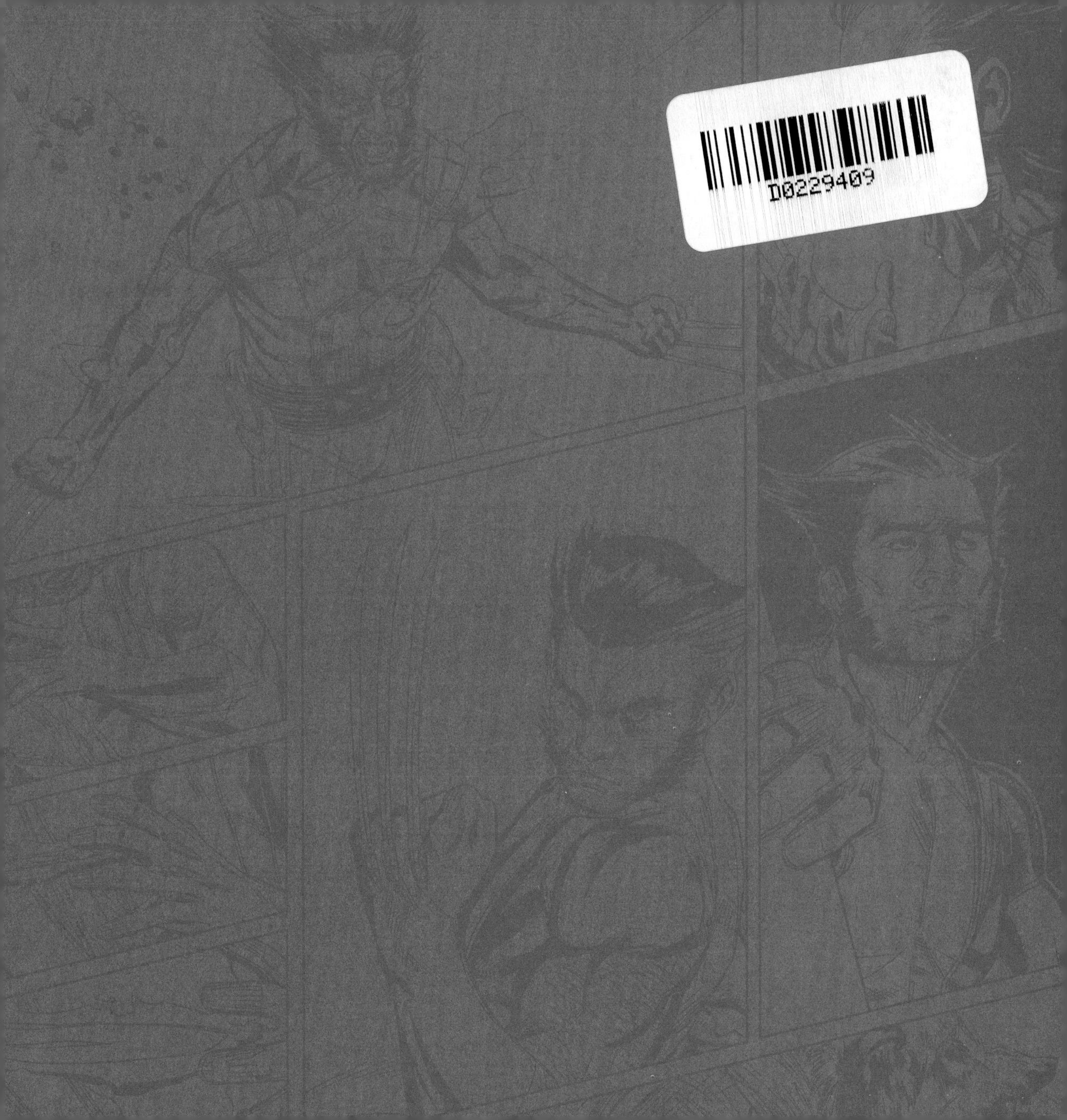

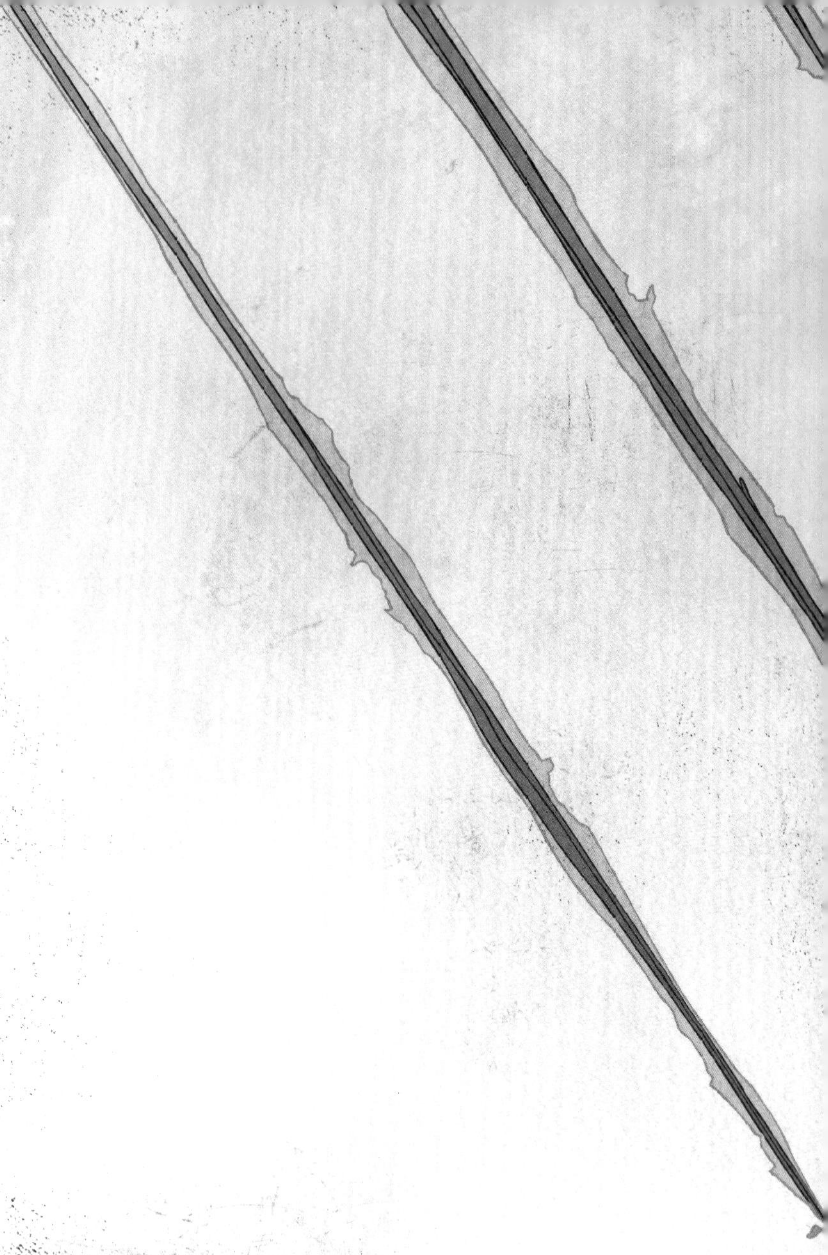

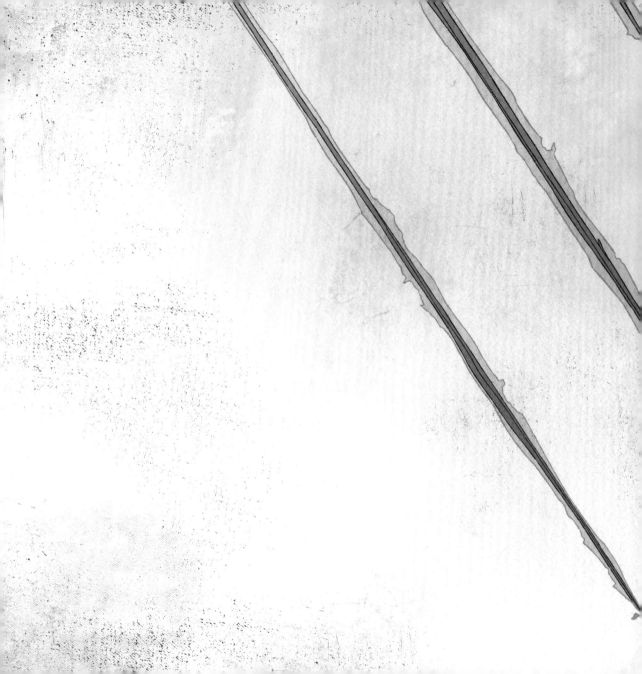

INSIGHT LEGENDS

MARVEL

THE WORLD ACCORDING TO

WOLVERINE

WRITTEN BY **MATTHEW K. MANNING**

ILLUSTRATED BY **STEPHEN MOONEY**

BANTAM
PRESS

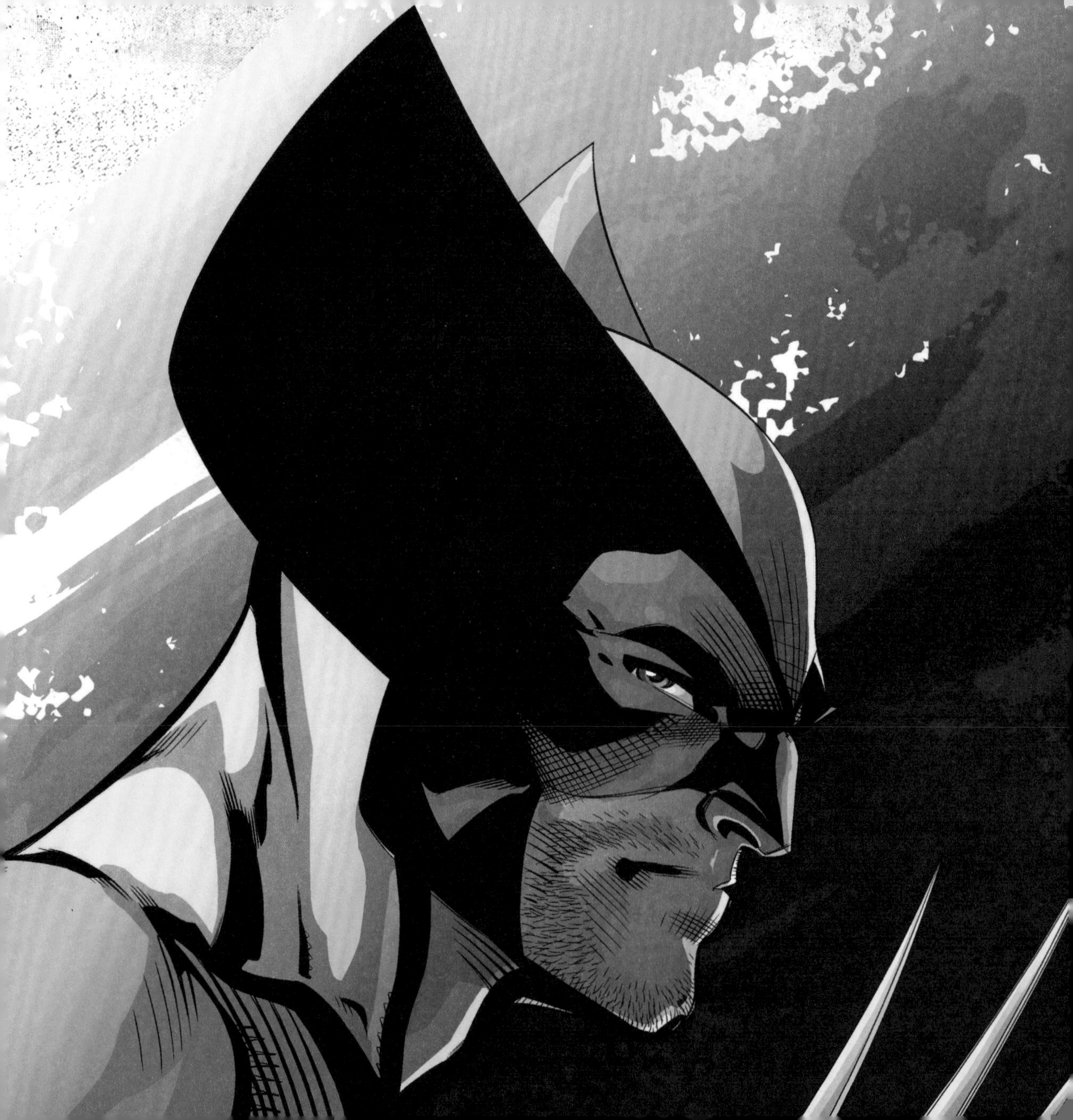

CONTENTS

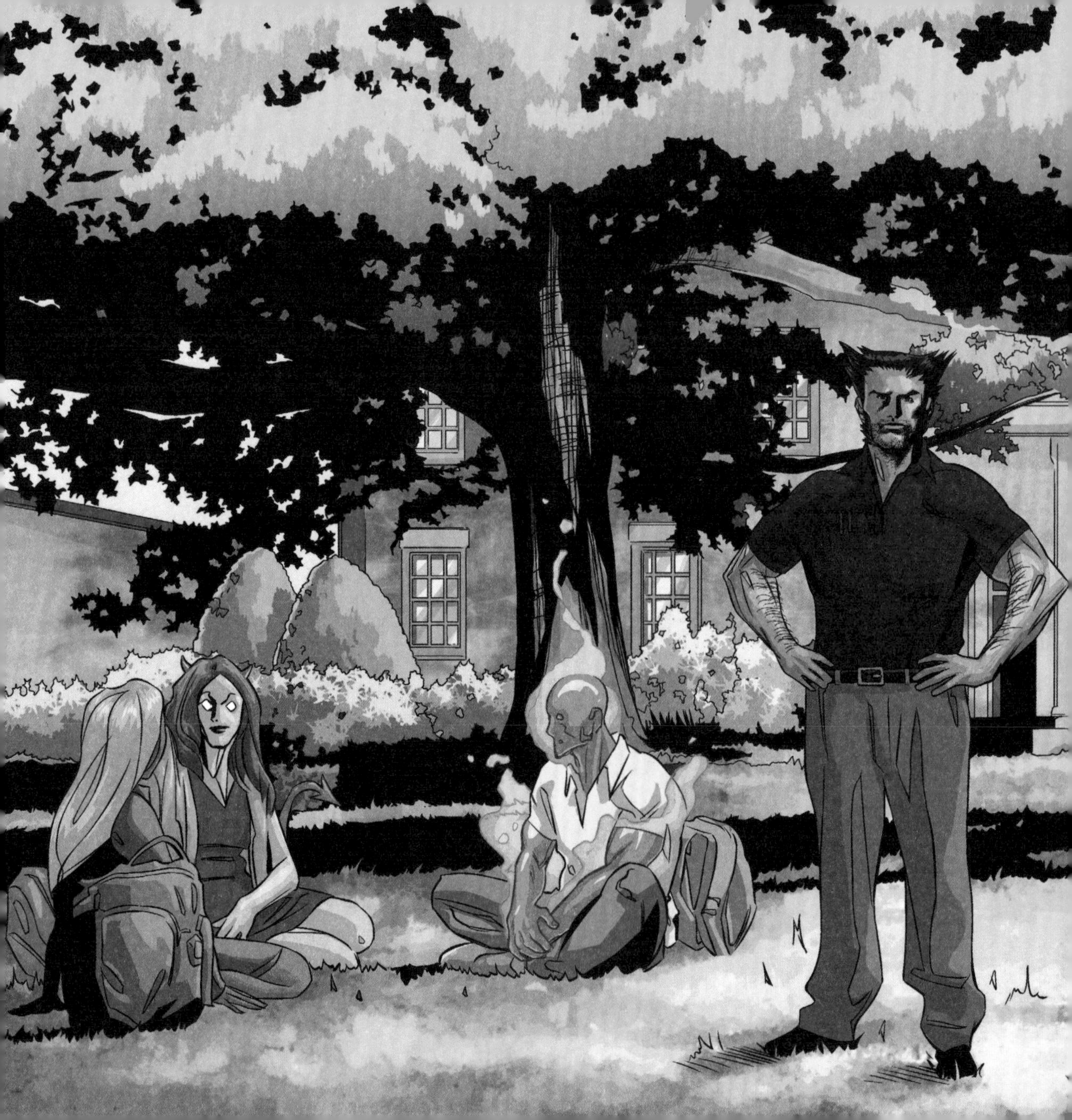

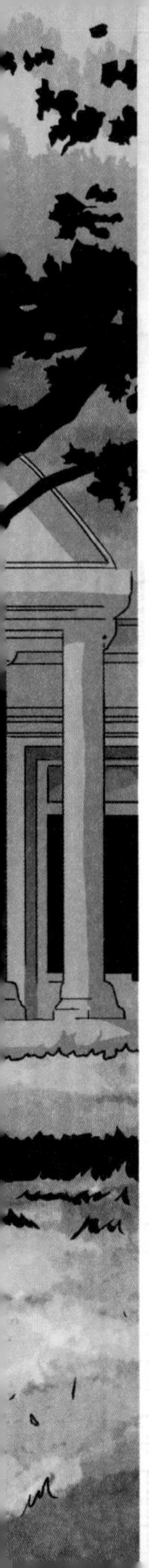

INTRODUCTION

I WANNA SAY RIGHT OFF THE BAT that this ain't exactly my sort of thing. I'm the kind of guy who likes to keep his thoughts to himself. Putting them all down like this, like I'm writing some sort of advice column in the part of the paper that no one worth his salt actually reads, well, it's gonna take some getting used to.

But I'm not doing this for me. This is for you kids. Or at least that's the idea.

If you're reading this, then odds are you're one of my students here at the school for mutants. Lately I've been doing my best to fill Charlie Xavier's shoes as headmaster. You all, you're a whole generation of kids with super powers looking to me to tell you how to live your lives. Sort of scary when you think about it. I'm not what most people would call a role model.

Thing is, I've been around for way longer than I have any right to. I've been a weapon, a hunter, a Super Hero. The whole nine. And it wasn't until I took over here at the Jean Grey School for Higher Learning that I started feeling like a grown-up. Feeling like I'm doing something actually worth doing.

You kids, most of you are like I was. You got an axe to grind, and nature went ahead and sharpened it for you. Gave you the ability to shoot lasers from your eyes or cut metal with your teeth. Truth is, you need somebody to look up to before you blow up some convenience store or shoot up a post office. You need to learn how to take the high road, even if you got to hear it from someone who spent way too much time down the other path.

So that's why I'm writing this book. I'm getting all my ideas out and on paper while I still can. Telling a little of my life story. Maybe I'll pass this thing out in your classes when I'm done writing it. Or maybe it won't ever leave my desk drawer.

In the world we live in, nothing lasts for long. I can't predict what messed up thing is gonna happen to you all tomorrow. All I can do is tell you how I got by and hope my story scares you away from doing anything too stupid. Or, at the very least, I hope my advice helps you live through it when you do that same stupid thing anyway.

They say I'm the best there is at what I do. Guess it's time the world finds out why.

JEAN GREY SCHOOL FOR HIGHER LEARNING
SALEM CENTER, WESTCHESTER COUNTY, NEW YORK

ABOUT ME

ALL OF YOU SHOULD KNOW my name by now. Or one of them, at least. My mutant handle, what I've gone by for most my time with the X-Men, is Wolverine. I also go by Logan, a name given to me when I needed one.

See, I spent the majority of my life not knowing much about who I was. Seems trauma can do that to you. Well, trauma and a whole lot of bad seeds poking and prodding at your head. Not too long ago, all my memories came rushing back to me during one of those big scale fights us super-types are always getting into.

But I'm getting ahead of myself. I guess I should start at the beginning. My real name's James. James Howlett. I was born in Canada over a hundred years ago now. Yeah, I look pretty good for my age. That has something to do with me being born with an X-gene. Got myself a nice mutant healing ability among other things. It's come in more than a little handy in my line of work.

When I was a kid, though, I hadn't shown any signs of being a mutant. I was sick, weak, and had enough allergies to keep any number of pharmaceutical companies in business. But that didn't stop me from

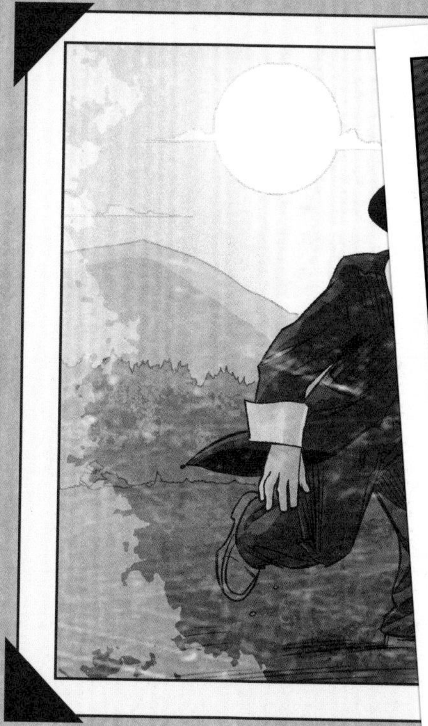

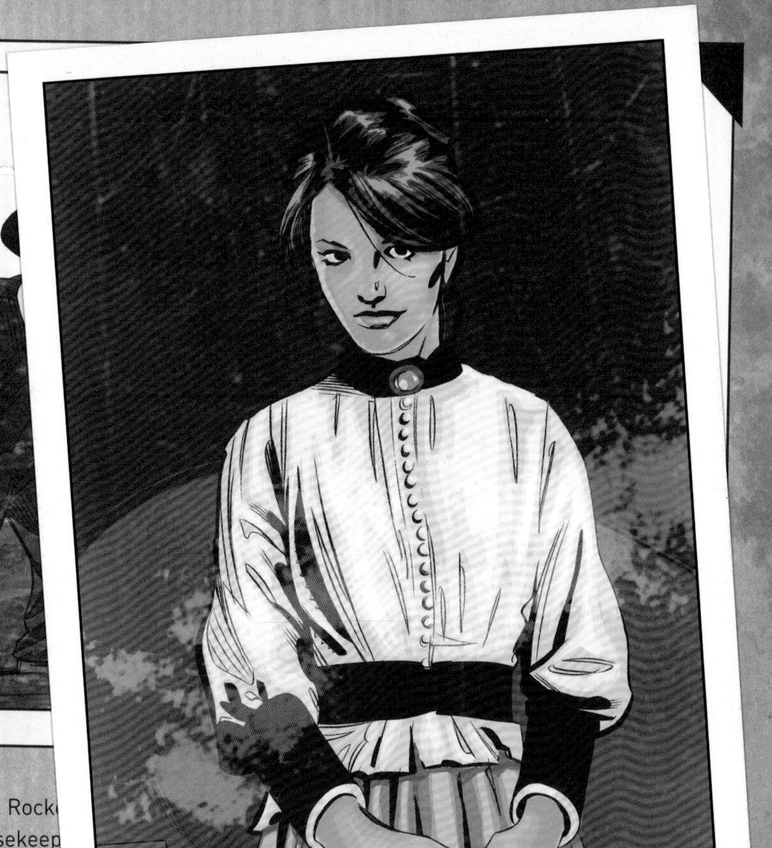

making a few friends. My dad was rich. Rocke
rich. Meant he could afford live-in housekeep
gardeners and the like. The gardener was a m
Logan, and his boy was a hotheaded kid name
and me got real close, and along with a red-he
on the house staff named Rose, we became so
like the Canadian version of the Three Musket

As it turns out, Logan wasn't much of a man. Took his anger out on his kid and turned Dog into the same kind of animal he was. Worse, it turned out that Logan was my real father, and I'm still not sure if that was something my mother had wanted or not. Things got heated the way things tend to do, and pretty soon Logan

animal, then took her own life. My grandfather saw what I was and disowned me. Kicked me out with only a few dollars to my name. But Rose, Rose stuck by me. We left together and she told folks my name was Logan, so my past would stay where it was.

Anyway, that's enough of that. I think you got a good enough idea now where I'm coming from.

SO YOU GOT ***POWERS?***

ALL RIGHT, SO YOU HEARD MY SOB STORY. Every mutant's got one. The world's tough out there for the likes of us, and for every accepting, tolerant person you meet, there's three who got a problem with the way you were born. Way I see it, powers ain't a blessing, and they ain't a curse. They're a little of both. And more important you're stuck with them.

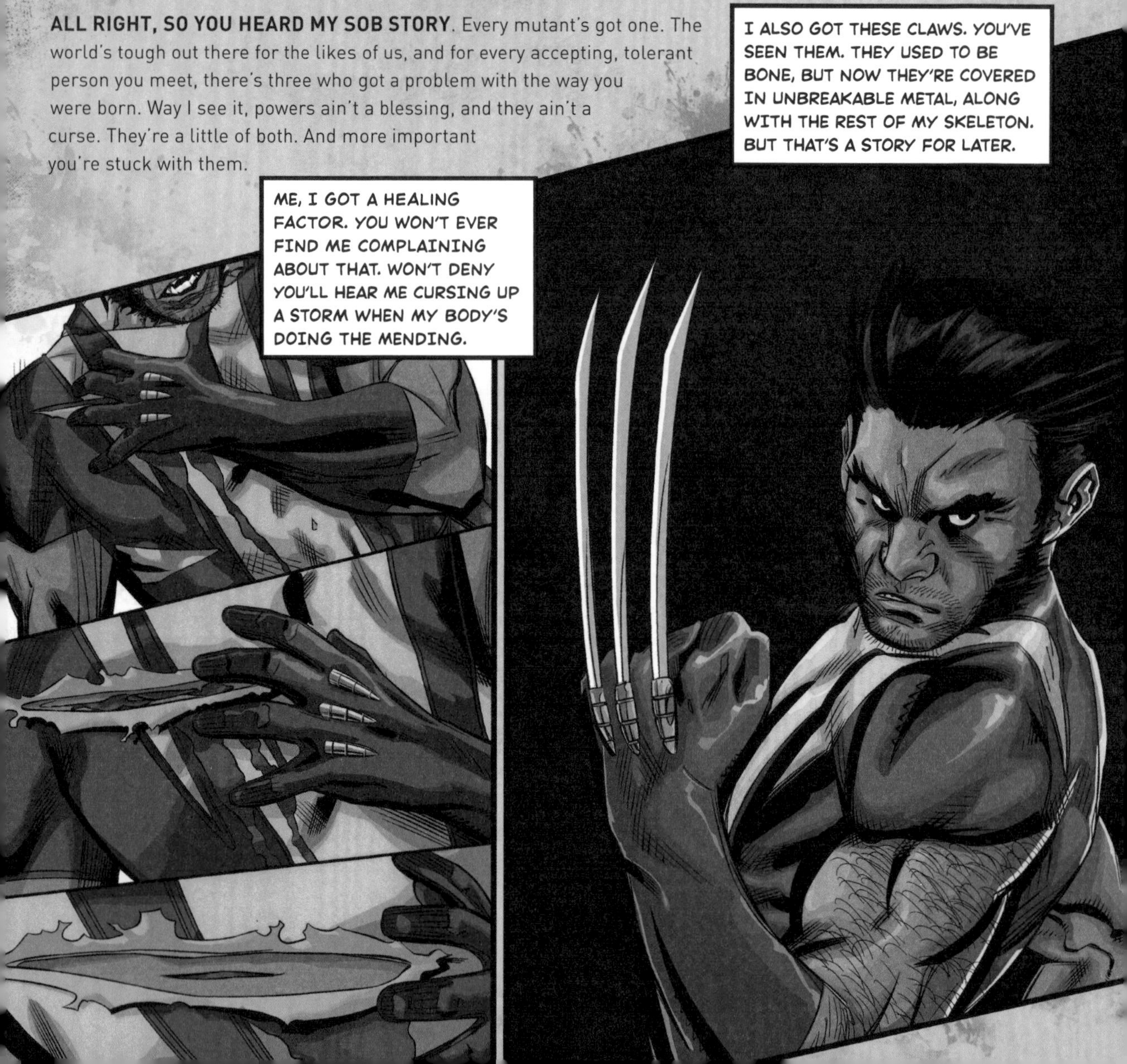
I ALSO GOT THESE CLAWS. YOU'VE SEEN THEM. THEY USED TO BE BONE, BUT NOW THEY'RE COVERED IN UNBREAKABLE METAL, ALONG WITH THE REST OF MY SKELETON. BUT THAT'S A STORY FOR LATER.
ME, I GOT A HEALING FACTOR. YOU WON'T EVER FIND ME COMPLAINING ABOUT THAT. WON'T DENY YOU'LL HEAR ME CURSING UP A STORM WHEN MY BODY'S DOING THE MENDING.

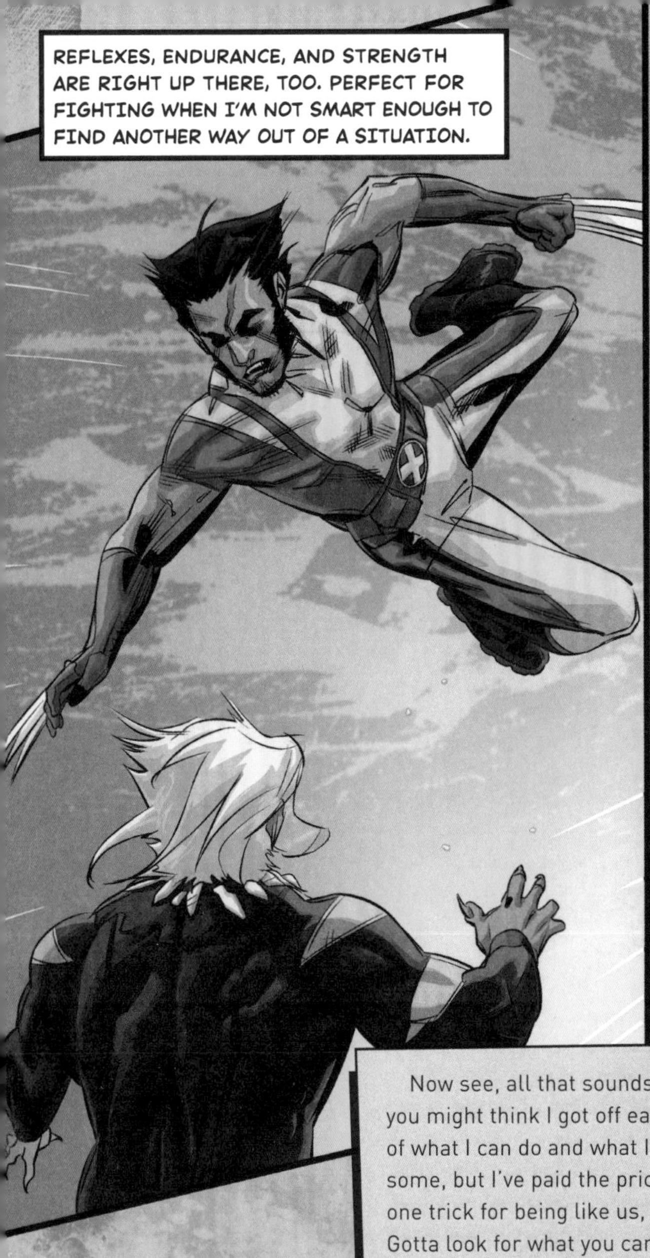
REFLEXES, ENDURANCE, AND STRENGTH ARE RIGHT UP THERE, TOO. PERFECT FOR FIGHTING WHEN I'M NOT SMART ENOUGH TO FIND ANOTHER WAY OUT OF A SITUATION.

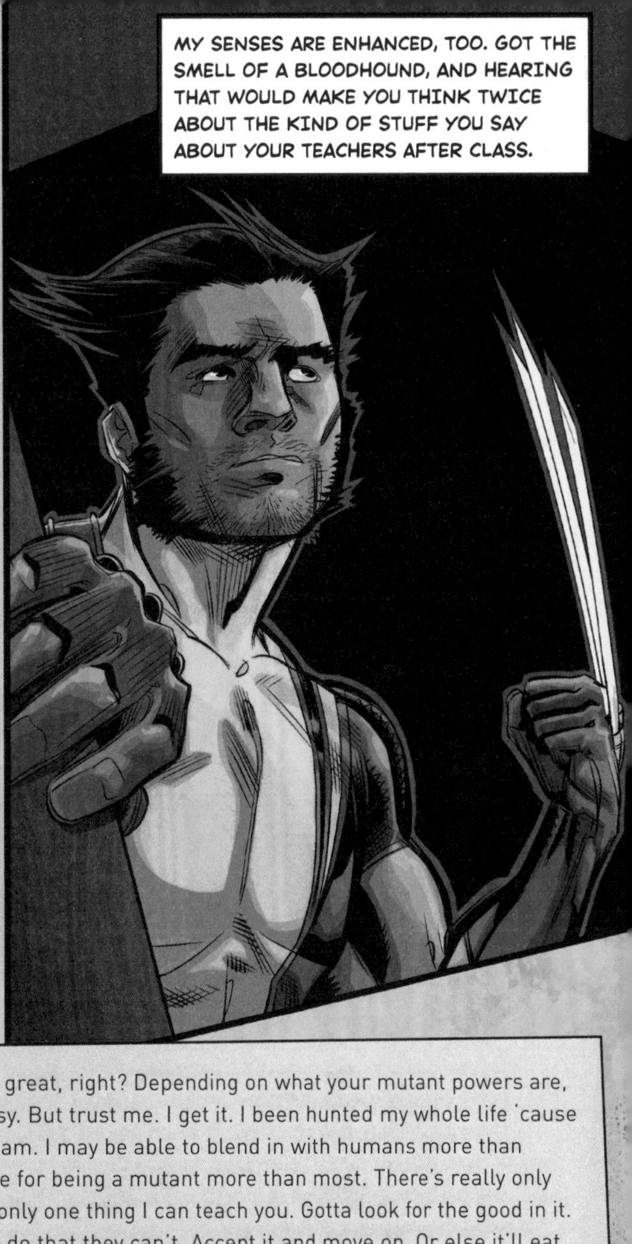
MY SENSES ARE ENHANCED, TOO. GOT THE SMELL OF A BLOODHOUND, AND HEARING THAT WOULD MAKE YOU THINK TWICE ABOUT THE KIND OF STUFF YOU SAY ABOUT YOUR TEACHERS AFTER CLASS.

Now see, all that sounds great, right? Depending on what your mutant powers are, you might think I got off easy. But trust me. I get it. I been hunted my whole life 'cause of what I can do and what I am. I may be able to blend in with humans more than some, but I've paid the price for being a mutant more than most. There's really only one trick for being like us, only one thing I can teach you. Gotta look for the good in it. Gotta look for what you can do that they can't. Accept it and move on. Or else it'll eat you alive. You got enough enemies already. Don't need to pick a fight with yourself.

PAIN

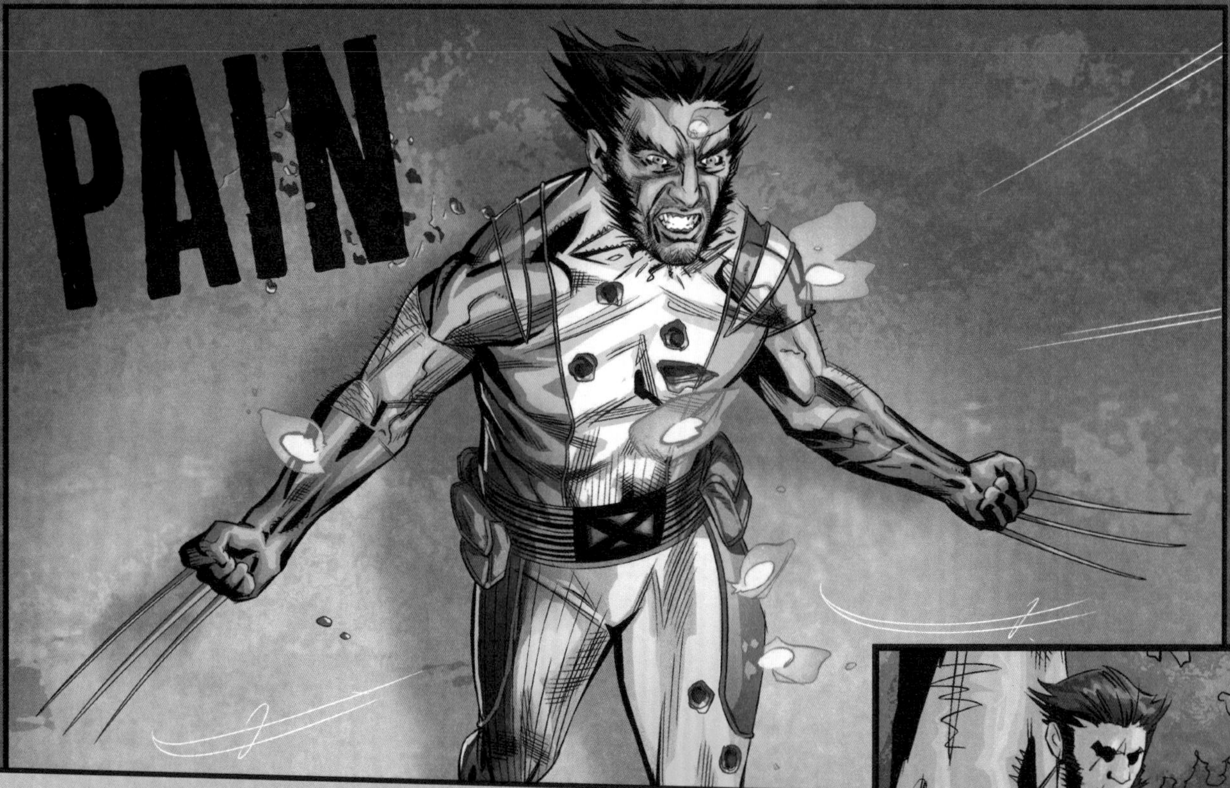

IT COMES WITH THE TERRITORY, and there ain't no getting around it. But here are a couple ways to deal with it.

My mutant healing factor's great. I'm one of the lucky ones when it comes to getting myself out of the trouble I've gotten myself into. I've fallen out of an airplane and walked away from it. But that doesn't mean it didn't hurt like hell.

See, for some reason my body doesn't feel the need to block out the pain when it's healing itself. I've felt every bullet, every cut, and every time my claws popped through my skin.

Sure, I'm more used to it now. But ask a diabetic if he likes pricking his finger every day. It's necessary, but it ain't the highlight of my evening, that's for sure.

There's a lot of talk out there about training your brain not to notice when your body's hurting. I've seen some use meditation to numb a wound, but it's not got the greatest track record for me. Sure, meditation has been a big part of my life for controlling the animal I got pacing right behind my eyes, but for pain management, I'm not a big fan.

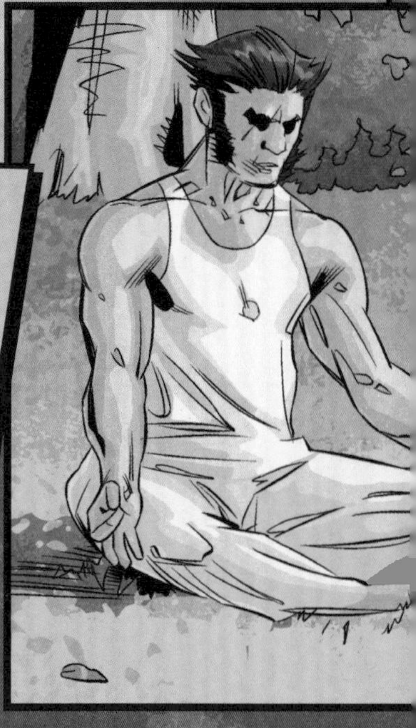

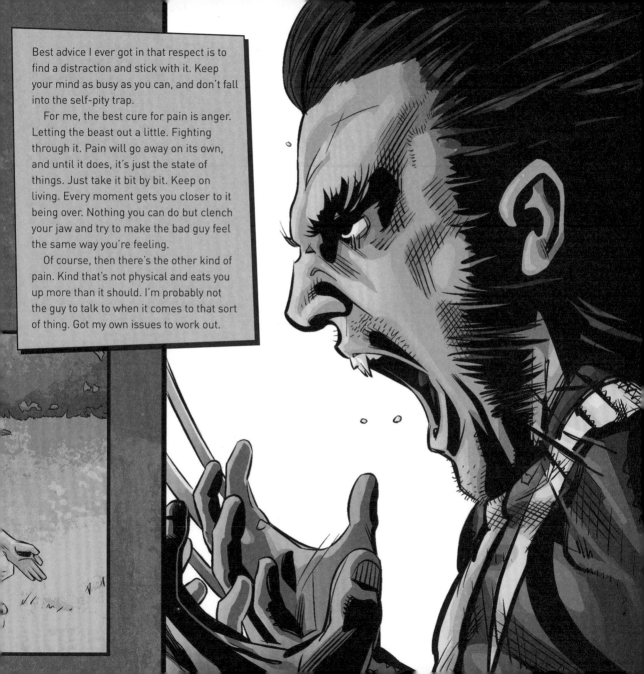

Best advice I ever got in that respect is to find a distraction and stick with it. Keep your mind as busy as you can, and don't fall into the self-pity trap.

For me, the best cure for pain is anger. Letting the beast out a little. Fighting through it. Pain will go away on its own, and until it does, it's just the state of things. Just take it bit by bit. Keep on living. Every moment gets you closer to it being over. Nothing you can do but clench your jaw and try to make the bad guy feel the same way you're feeling.

Of course, then there's the other kind of pain. Kind that's not physical and eats you up more than it should. I'm probably not the guy to talk to when it comes to that sort of thing. Got my own issues to work out.

HUNTING MADE EASY

BEFORE I GET STARTED, I know there are lots of you who may be against the idea of hunting. Killing ain't for everyone, whether it be taking the life of an animal for a meal or putting down the kind of animal that ain't gonna do anybody any good if it continues to be let loose in the world. But hunting ain't the same as killing. And if you're gonna live the life of an active mutant, you're gonna need to know how to hunt.

Now you'll learn the bulk of how to stalk, track, and trap your opponent in class. It'd take a whole lot more patience and paper than I got to teach you all the ins and outs of it right now. But what I am going to tell you is how I got started.

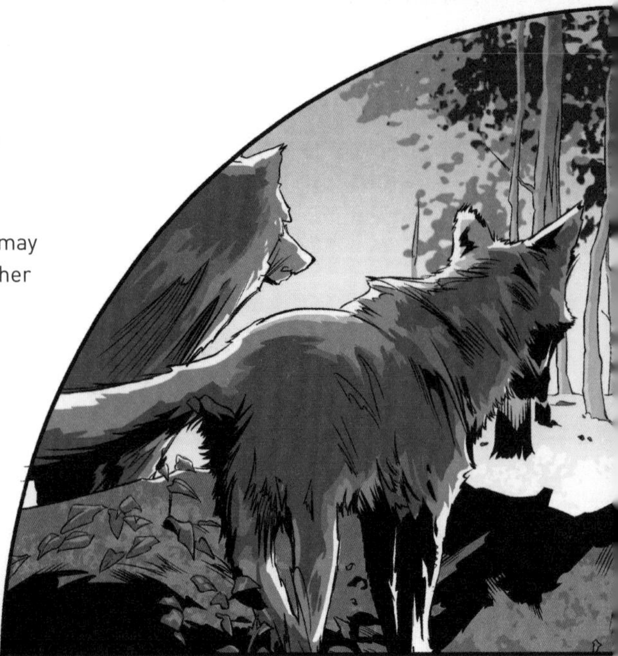

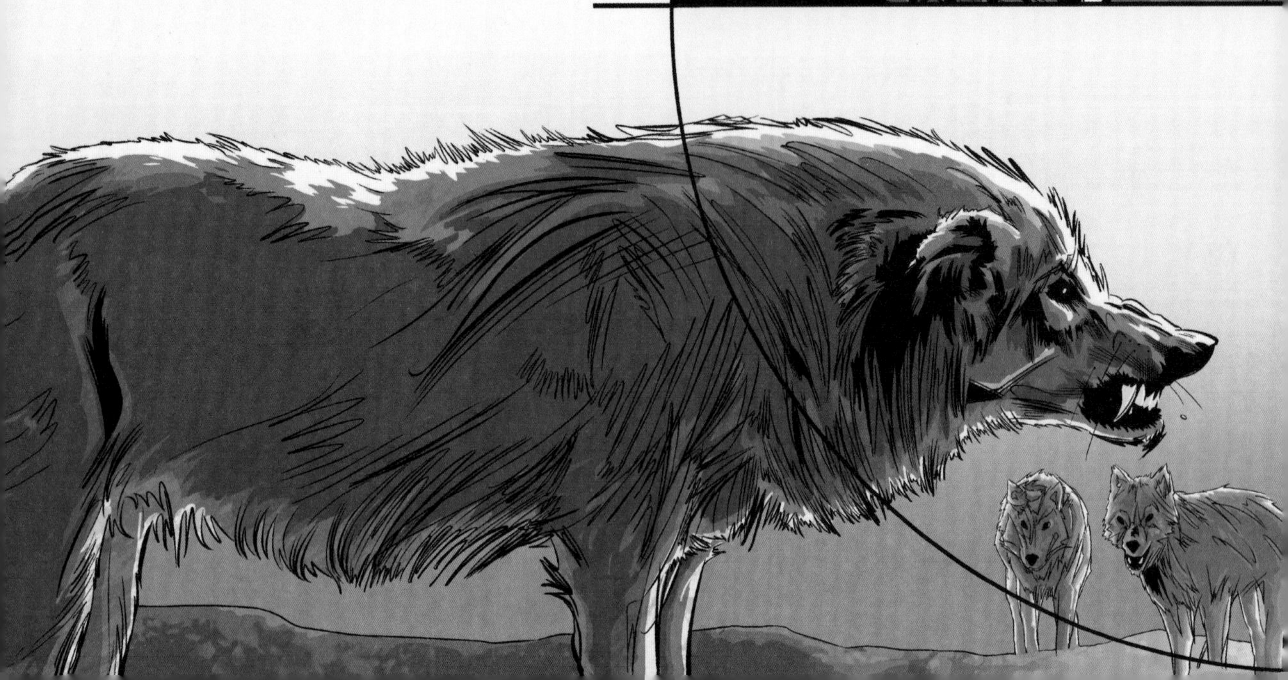

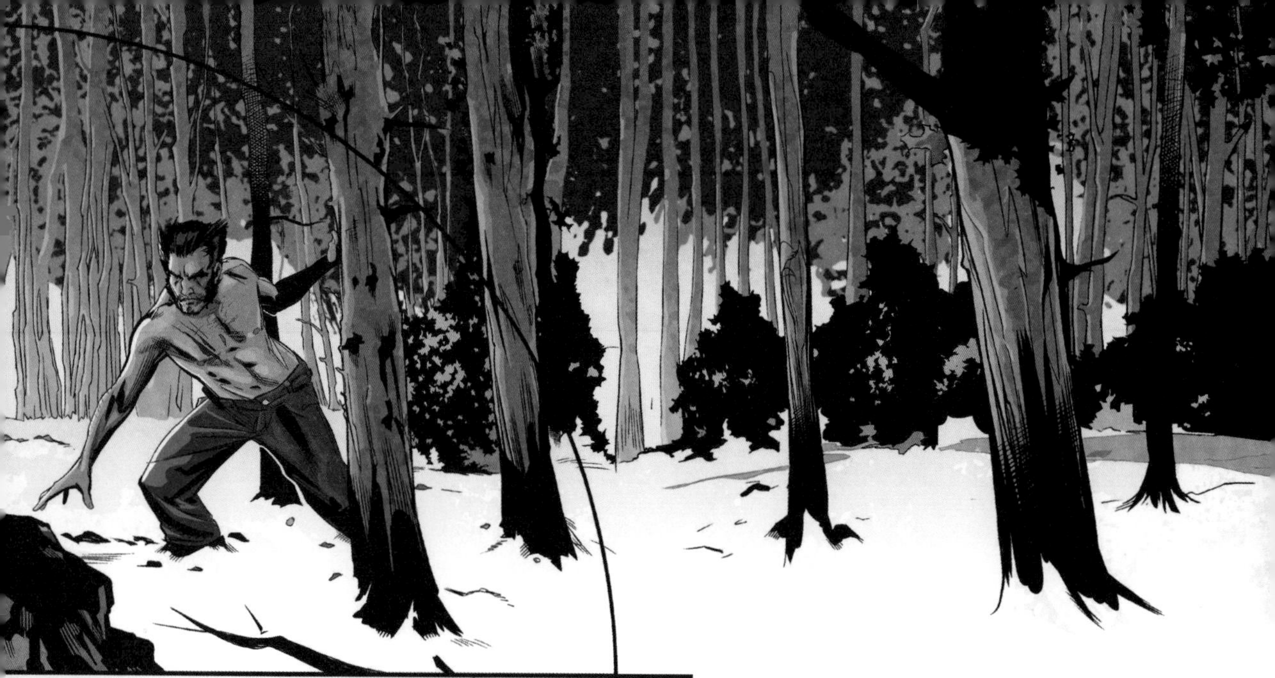

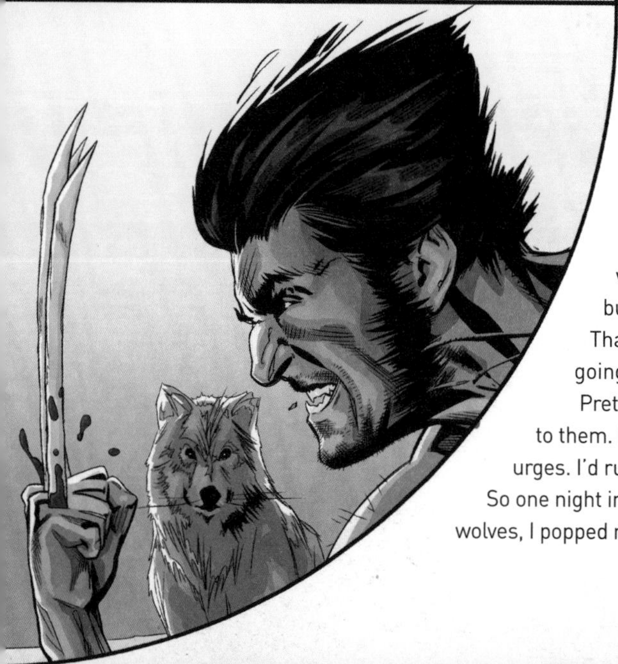

When I was a boy, I don't think I even had it in me to kill a housefly if one got into my room at night. I saw my father fight his battles with the help of other men, and then I saw what that got him: bleeding out on a rug that was worth more than most people's yearly salary.

After I was kicked out of my dad's place with only Rose by my side, I was pretty much no use to anybody. I couldn't figure out how to use my powers and couldn't make any sense of the world. So I went ahead and left it. I worked in a quarry up north but spent all my free time in the woods, listening and watching. That's 99 percent of hunting right there. Paying attention to what's going on around you. The stuff nobody else is paying attention to.

Pretty soon I was listening to my own instincts. But I couldn't commit to them. Not fully. I was scared of what was inside me. The claws. The urges. I'd run from any fight there was, until the day I got tired of running. So one night in the woods, when I found myself surrounded by a pack of hungry wolves, I popped my claws for the second time in my life. And I joined them.

KEEPING THE ANIMAL IN CHECK

BACK WHEN I WAS LIVING on the quarry with Rose, I spent my nights with the wolves. I was running in a pack, leading them soon enough. But the whole time, what I really wanted out of life was getting away from me. Rose . . . she was slipping away even before I lost her for good.

I was letting my anger keep me going, and that was a side of me Rose hated. A part of me knew that, but when Dog showed up back in my life—with a nice clawed scar across his face as a trophy of the night his father killed mine—I still decided to put him down. Rose being Rose got in the way of my claws, and . . . well, that night I left the quarry forever.

Back then, I had no desire to keep the beast under lock and key. I lived in the forest, roamed wherever the hunt took me. Earned a reputation. But soon enough, I started to realize I wasn't giving myself enough credit. I wasn't a dumb animal, and I needed to stop hiding like one.

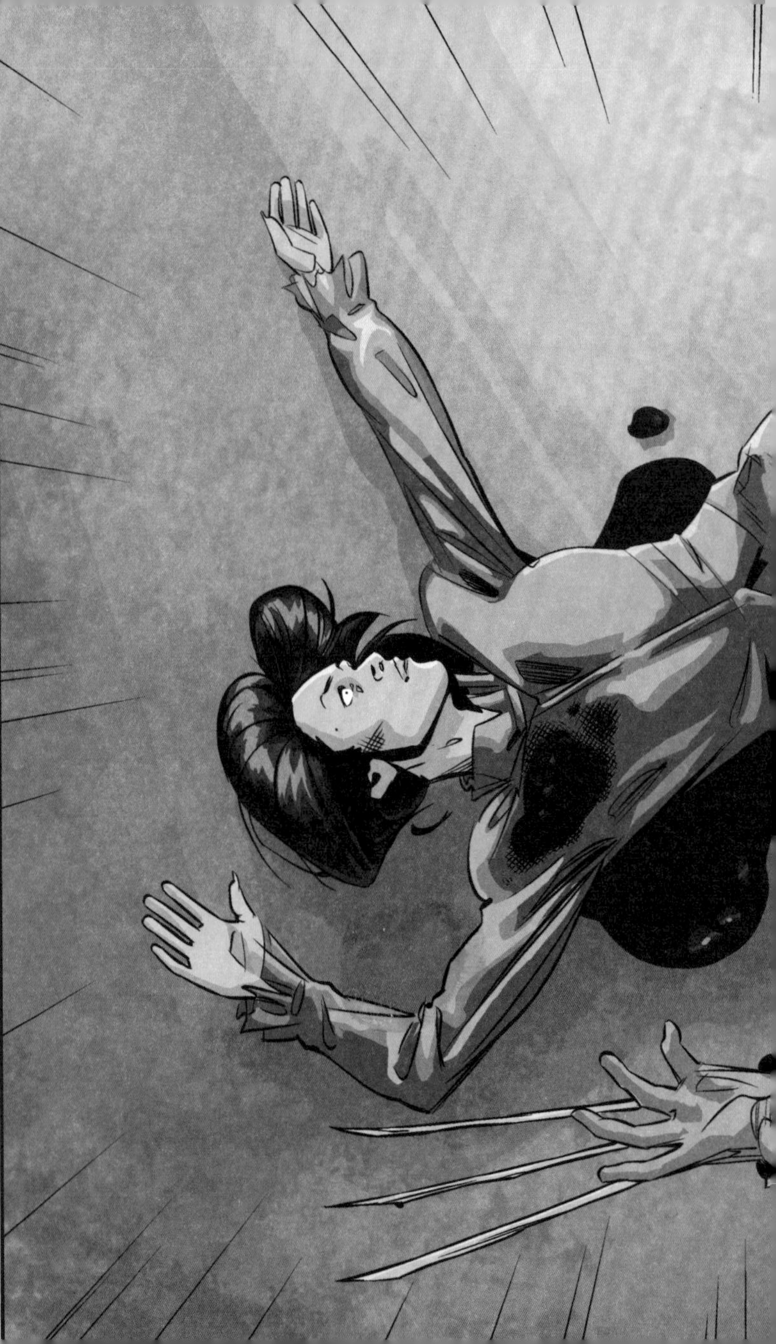

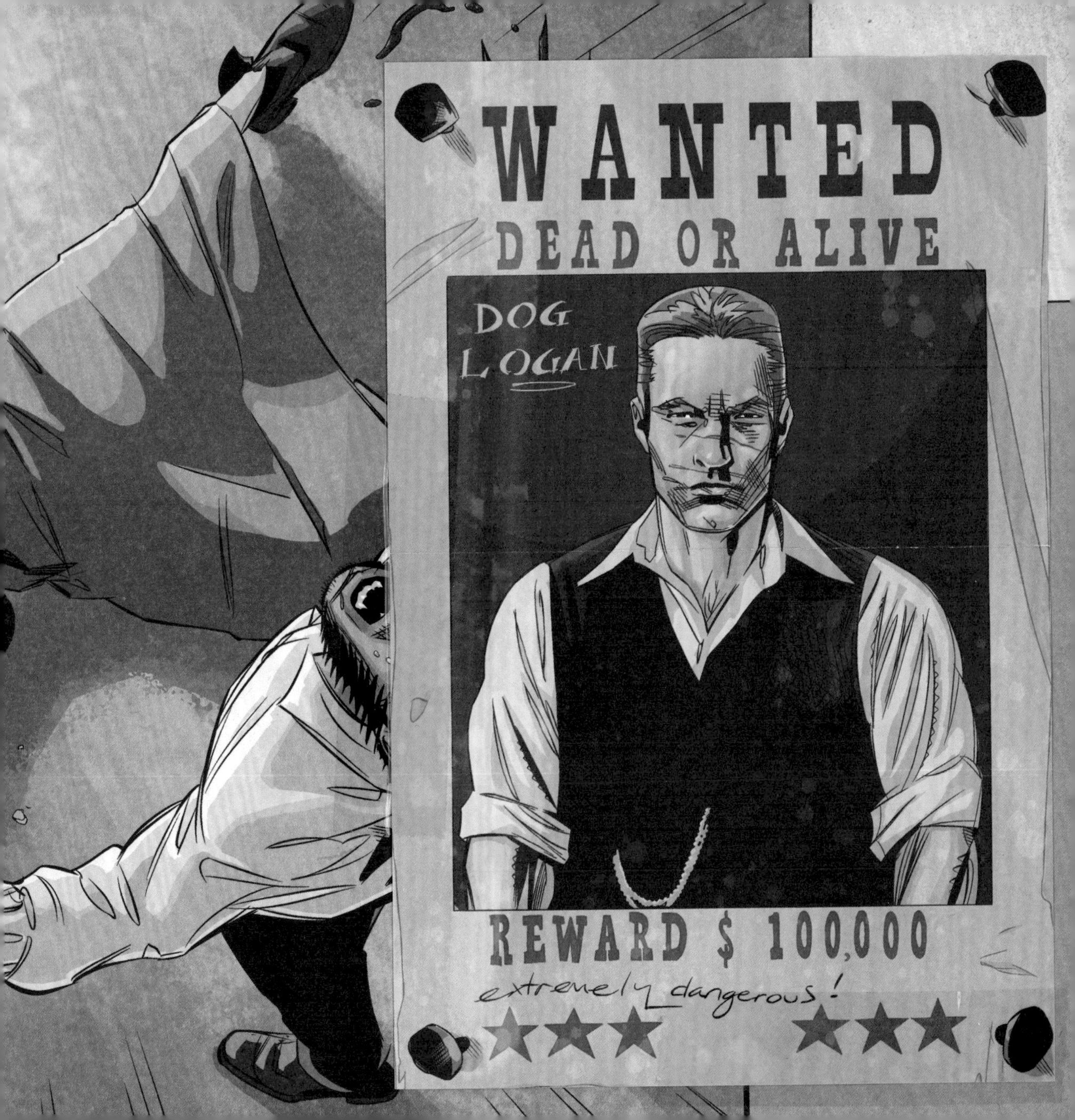
WANTED
DEAD OR ALIVE
DOG
LOGAN
REWARD $ 100,000
extremely dangerous!

LIVING OFF THE LAND

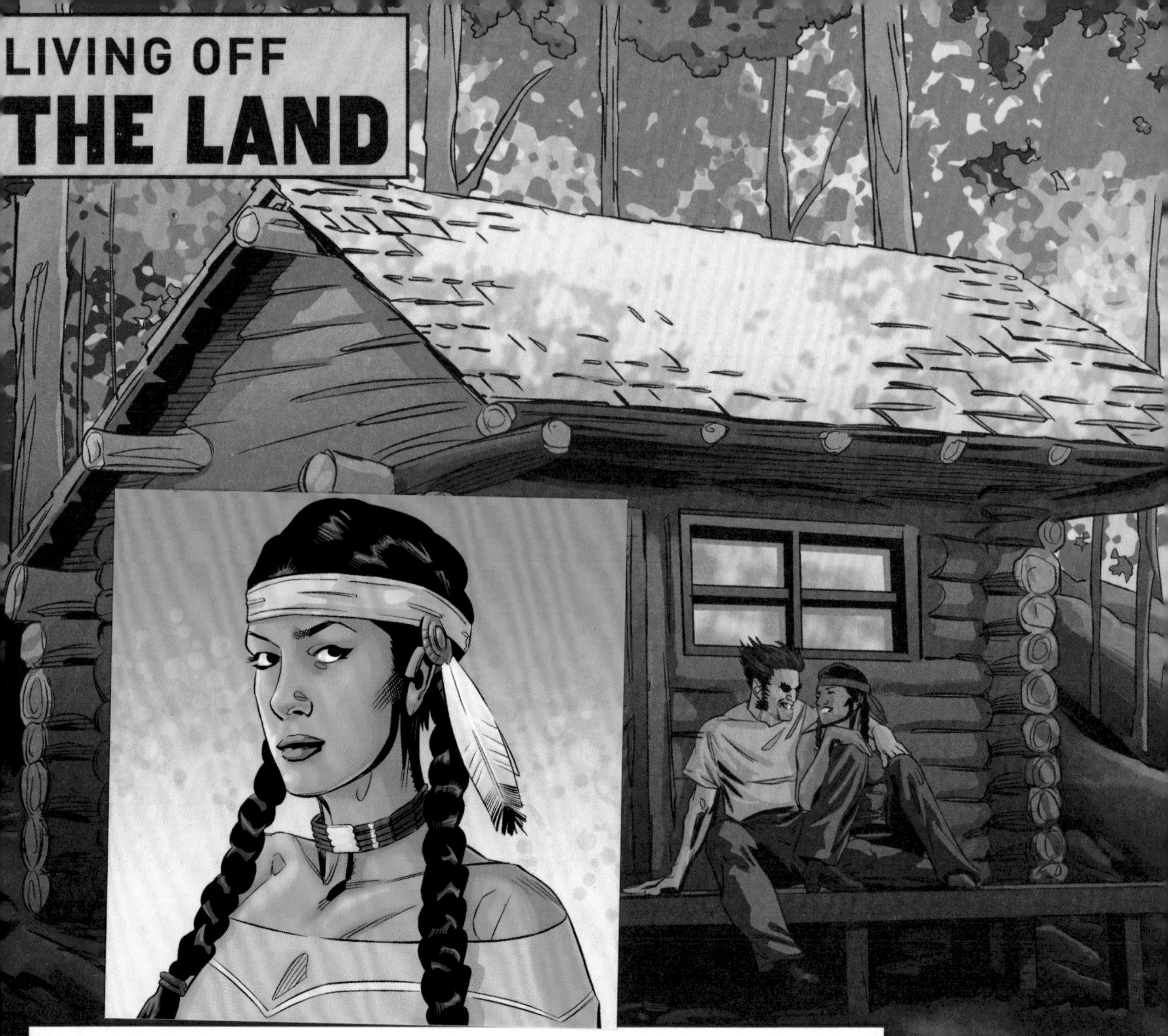

WHEN THINGS GET TO ME TOO MUCH, I ain't a fan of sticking around and just taking it. This is a great big world, and there's a little corner of happiness for all of us out there. I found mine in Canada with a member of the Blackfoot tribe named Silver Fox. For a time, we lived in a small cabin that I had the privilege of building myself. Fox, she helped me forget my past. And I'm telling you, when you get a chance to live a life like that, you snatch that up.

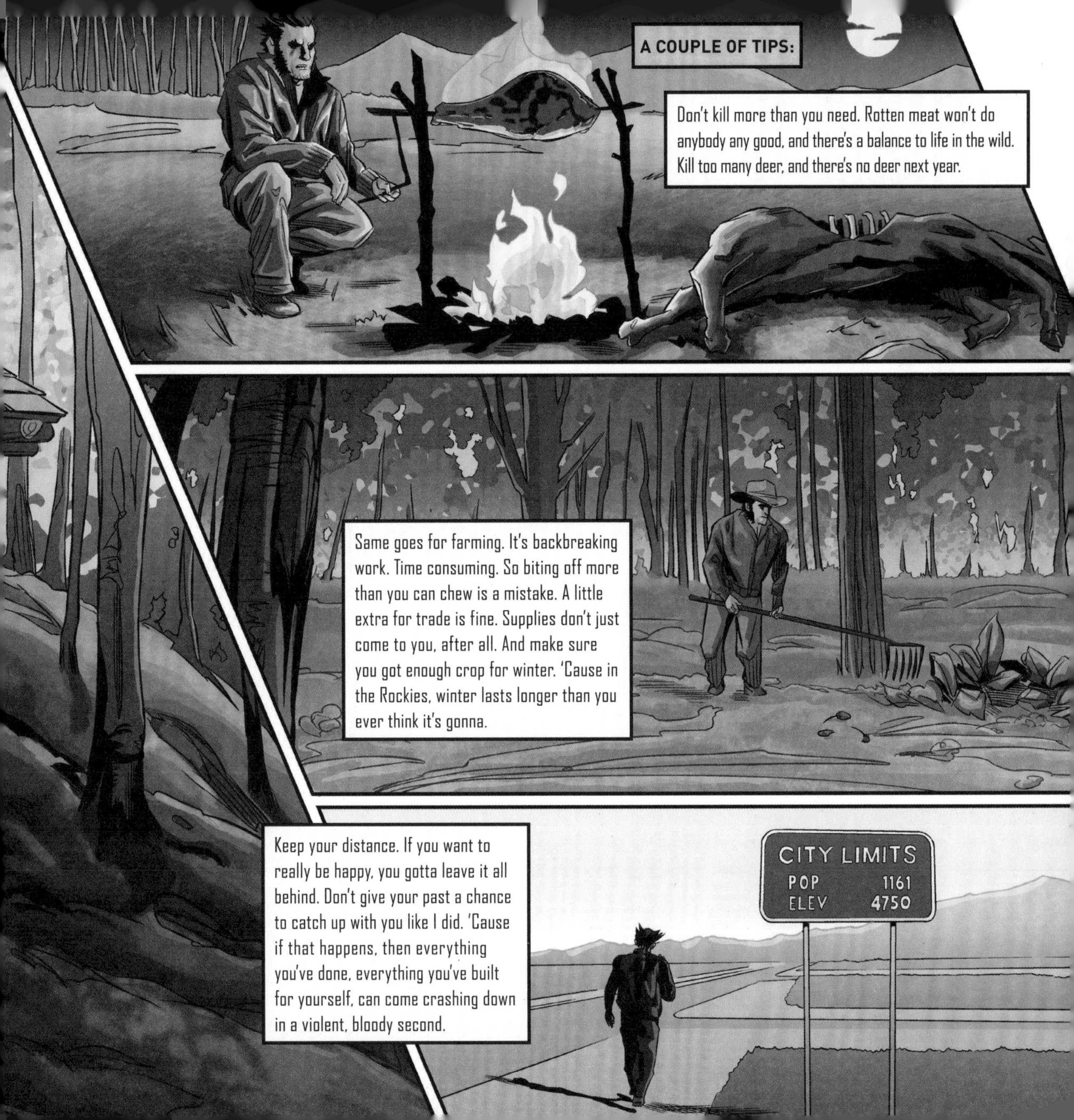
A COUPLE OF TIPS:
Don't kill more than you need. Rotten meat won't do anybody any good, and there's a balance to life in the wild. Kill too many deer, and there's no deer next year.
Same goes for farming. It's backbreaking work. Time consuming. So biting off more than you can chew is a mistake. A little extra for trade is fine. Supplies don't just come to you, after all. And make sure you got enough crop for winter. 'Cause in the Rockies, winter lasts longer than you ever think it's gonna.
Keep your distance. If you want to really be happy, you gotta leave it all behind. Don't give your past a chance to catch up with you like I did. 'Cause if that happens, then everything you've done, everything you've built for yourself, can come crashing down in a violent, bloody second.
CITY LIMITS
POP 1161
ELEV 4750

TELLING FRIENDS FROM ENEMIES

NO MATTER HOW HARD A MAN TRIES to keep his head down and mind his own business, there will always be those who find some sort of power in breaking that man down any way they can. More often than not, those that want to do you the most harm are those you have the most in common with. And it's important to be able to pick out the bad eggs as soon as you see them. They stick around for long, and things'll start to stink.

Turns out I'm part of some ancient breed of feral mutants calling themselves the Lupine. Trouble is, there's more of them around than I originally thought. And not all of them share my sunny disposition.

One of the worst of the bunch is Victor Creed, a man who calls himself Sabretooth. I knew we were alike when I first spotted him in Tokyo, but the fact that he was busy killing innocent girls tipped me off right away that we weren't fated to be "besties." I stopped him that day and made a lifelong

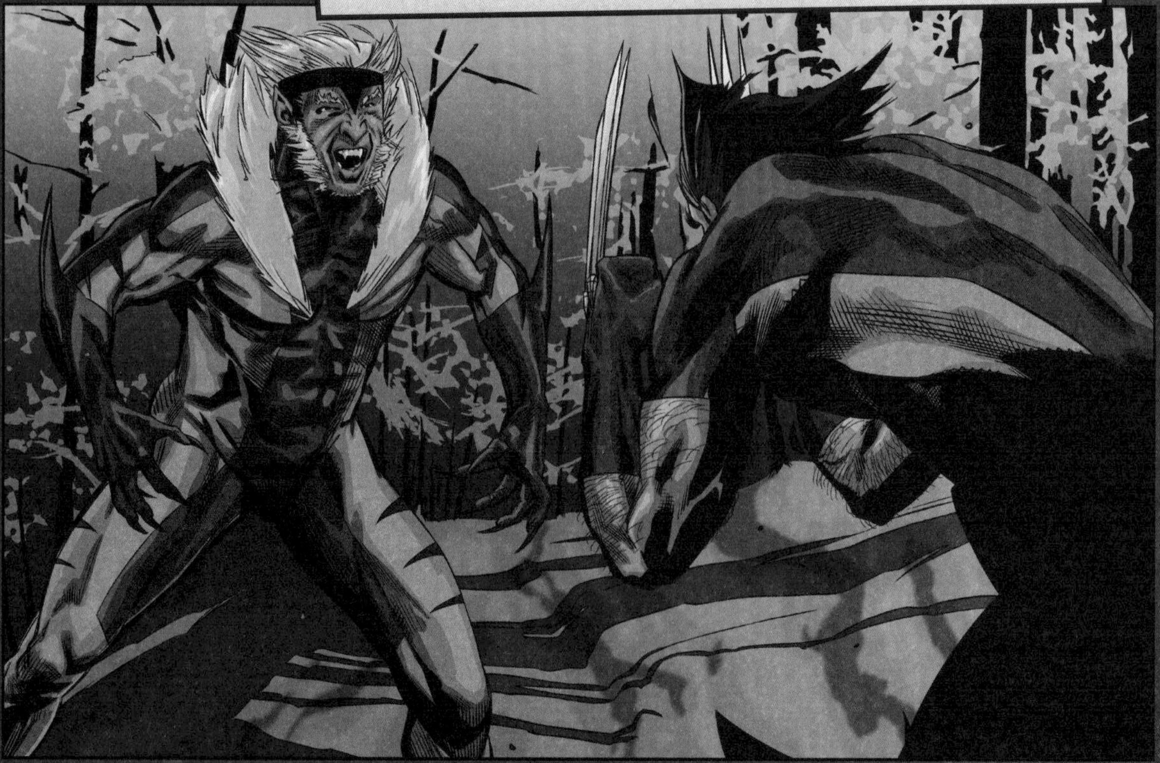

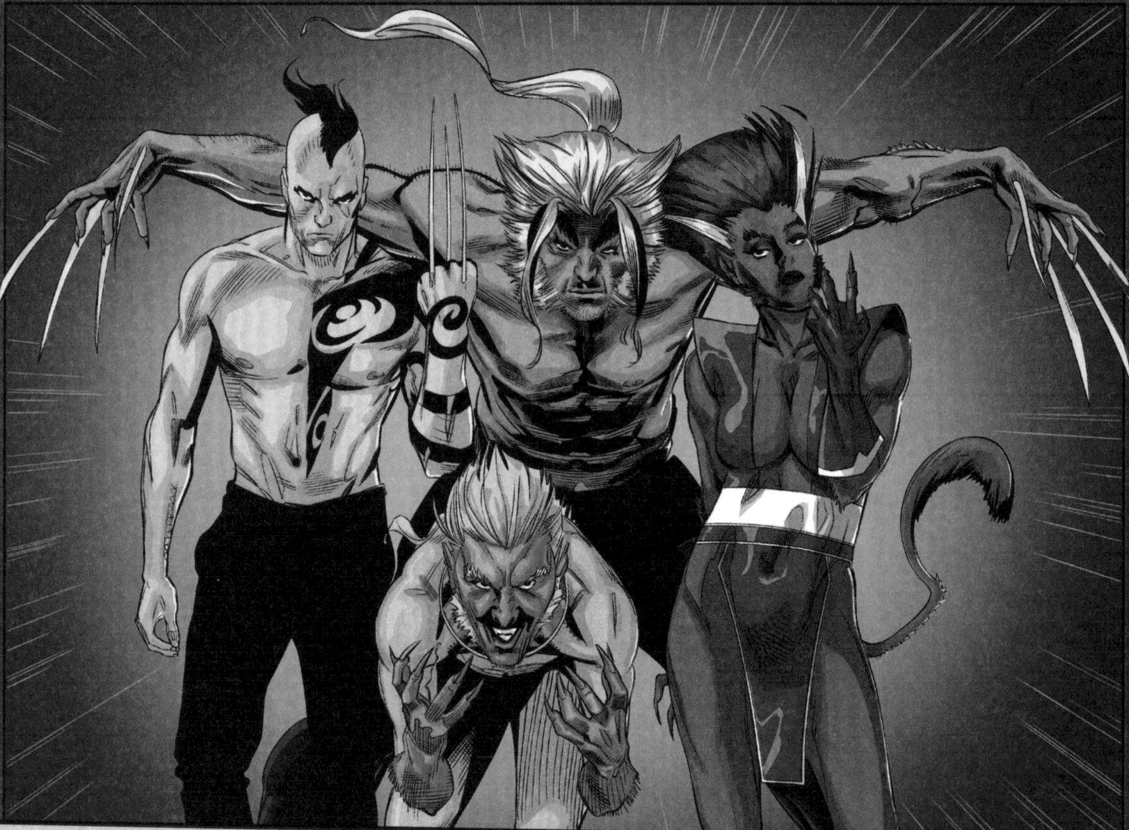

enemy in the process. And he made one right back not too long afterward when he found my little peace of heaven with Silver Fox and turned it into hell. Grudges don't fade away for our kind, and thanks to Sabretooth, I'll always have the memory of returning home to that cabin to find Fox on the floor lifeless, with the words "Happy Birthday" spelled out in blood on a nearby wall.

As bad as Creed is, he was just the puppet. There was a bigger threat waiting behind the scenes, as he had for centuries. His name was Romulus, the first Lupine. A man obsessed with the need to manipulate and control the rest of us. It was Romulus who ordered the hit on Silver Fox to get me under his control. And through a whole mess of brainwashing, he did just that.

For years I worked for this man who should have been my enemy. Never questioning it like I should have. I did all kinds of things I'm ashamed of, and all because I thought that this was the way a natural-born killer like me was supposed to act.

Before you work with a man, any man, you look him in the eyes. If you see the worst side of yourself looking right back, then that's not the guy you want to be fighting alongside.

ON THE ROAD

SEEMS MY WHOLE LIFE I been looking to the road to clear my head and escape my troubles. Travel can be good for doing just that and gaining a new perspective on things you might already think you're sure about. So here's some tips for life on the move:

Live cheap. Don't ask for much and don't look for much. You ain't gonna get by for long demanding five-star meals and

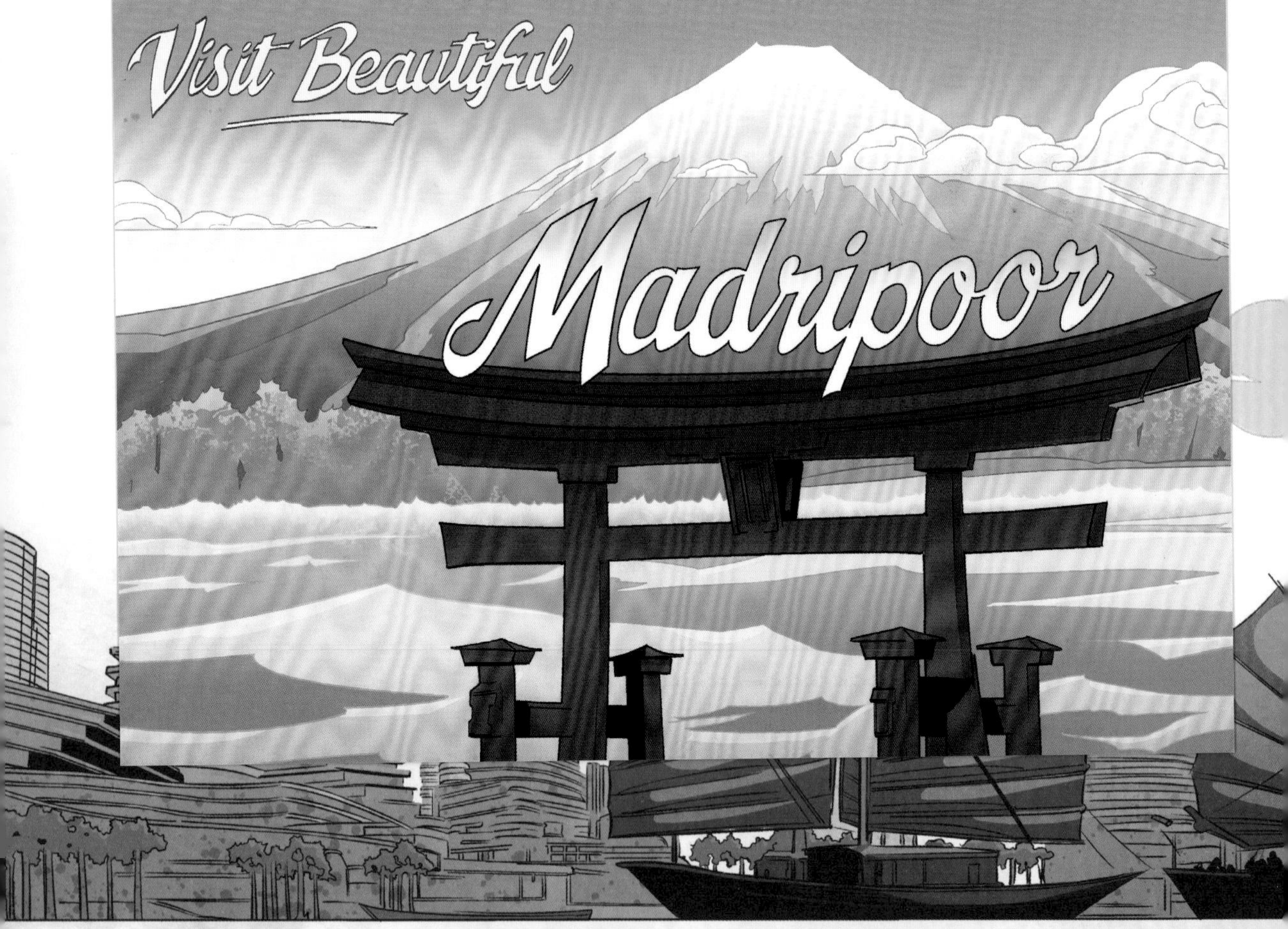
Visit Beautiful
Madripoor

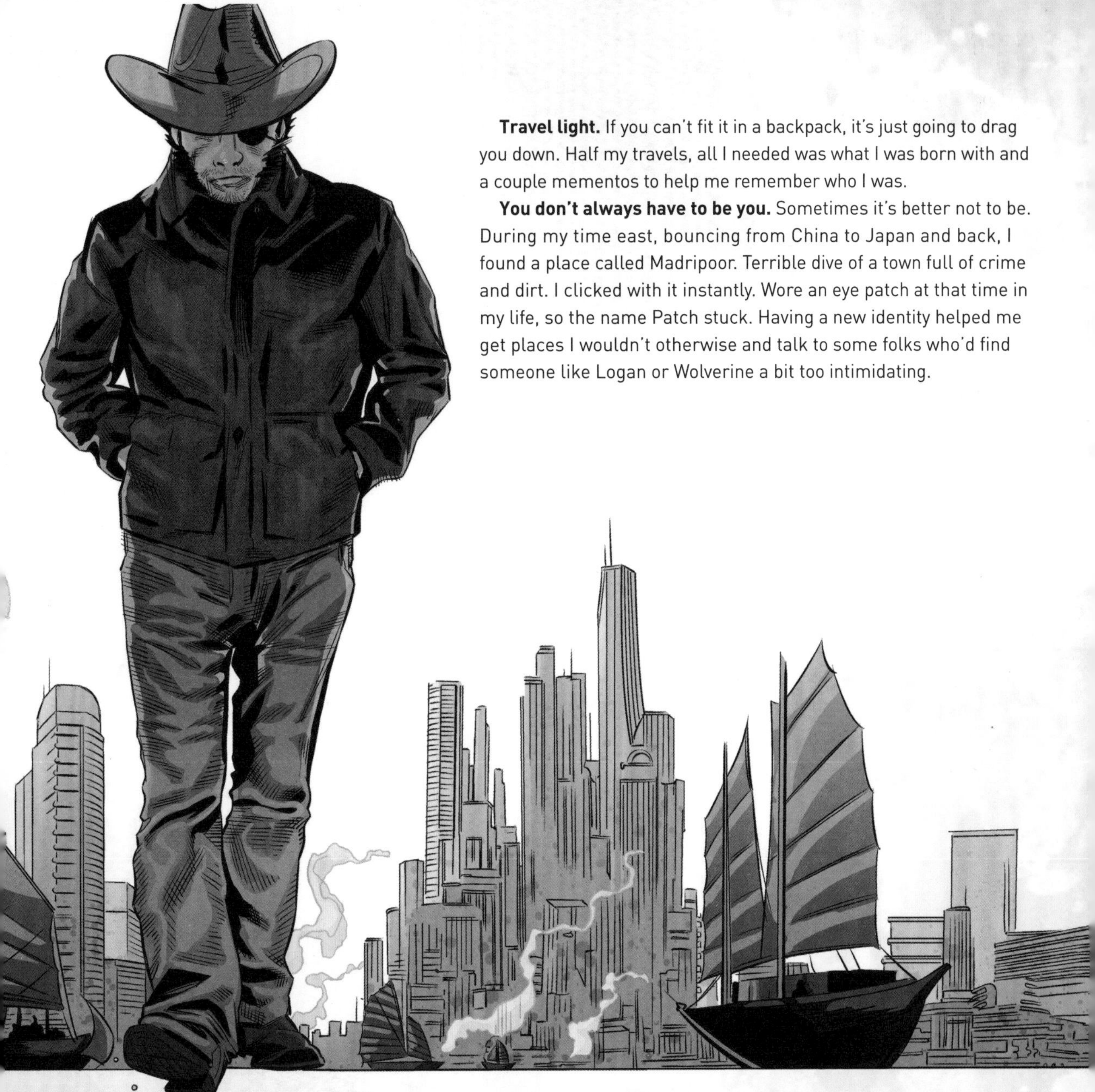

Travel light. If you can't fit it in a backpack, it's just going to drag you down. Half my travels, all I needed was what I was born with and a couple mementos to help me remember who I was.

You don't always have to be you. Sometimes it's better not to be. During my time east, bouncing from China to Japan and back, I found a place called Madripoor. Terrible dive of a town full of crime and dirt. I clicked with it instantly. Wore an eye patch at that time in my life, so the name Patch stuck. Having a new identity helped me get places I wouldn't otherwise and talk to some folks who'd find someone like Logan or Wolverine a bit too intimidating.

TAKING
ORDERS

WHETHER IT'S IN A SUPER HERO THROWDOWN or fighting the Nazis during a big, fat war, sometimes you gotta just put your ego in check and listen to guys smarter than you. Ain't nothing wrong with that, but there's a couple things you need to keep in mind when it's your turn to play soldier.

Don't follow directions blindly. Find out why they want you to do what you're about to do before you do it. You're not gonna get take-backs, and some things can't be undone. Think it through before you act.

You know the old saying about things being too good to be true. You get orders that indulge the worst side of you and justify you acting the way you shouldn't, you know it's time to walk away. After Silver Fox was killed, Sabretooth and Romulus convinced me to let loose my rage on the nearest town. I was little more than a wild beast doing the bidding of the men I should've been trying to kill. And all because it felt good to let the animal out, even if deep down I knew there was a reason I had it caged in the first place.

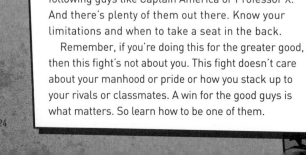

If you're honest, you know the guys who are better at this than you. You know the guys with better morals and brains. You'll never have a problem following guys like Captain America or Professor X. And there's plenty of them out there. Know your limitations and when to take a seat in the back.

Remember, if you're doing this for the greater good, then this fight's not about you. This fight doesn't care about your manhood or pride or how you stack up to your rivals or classmates. A win for the good guys is what matters. So learn how to be one of them.

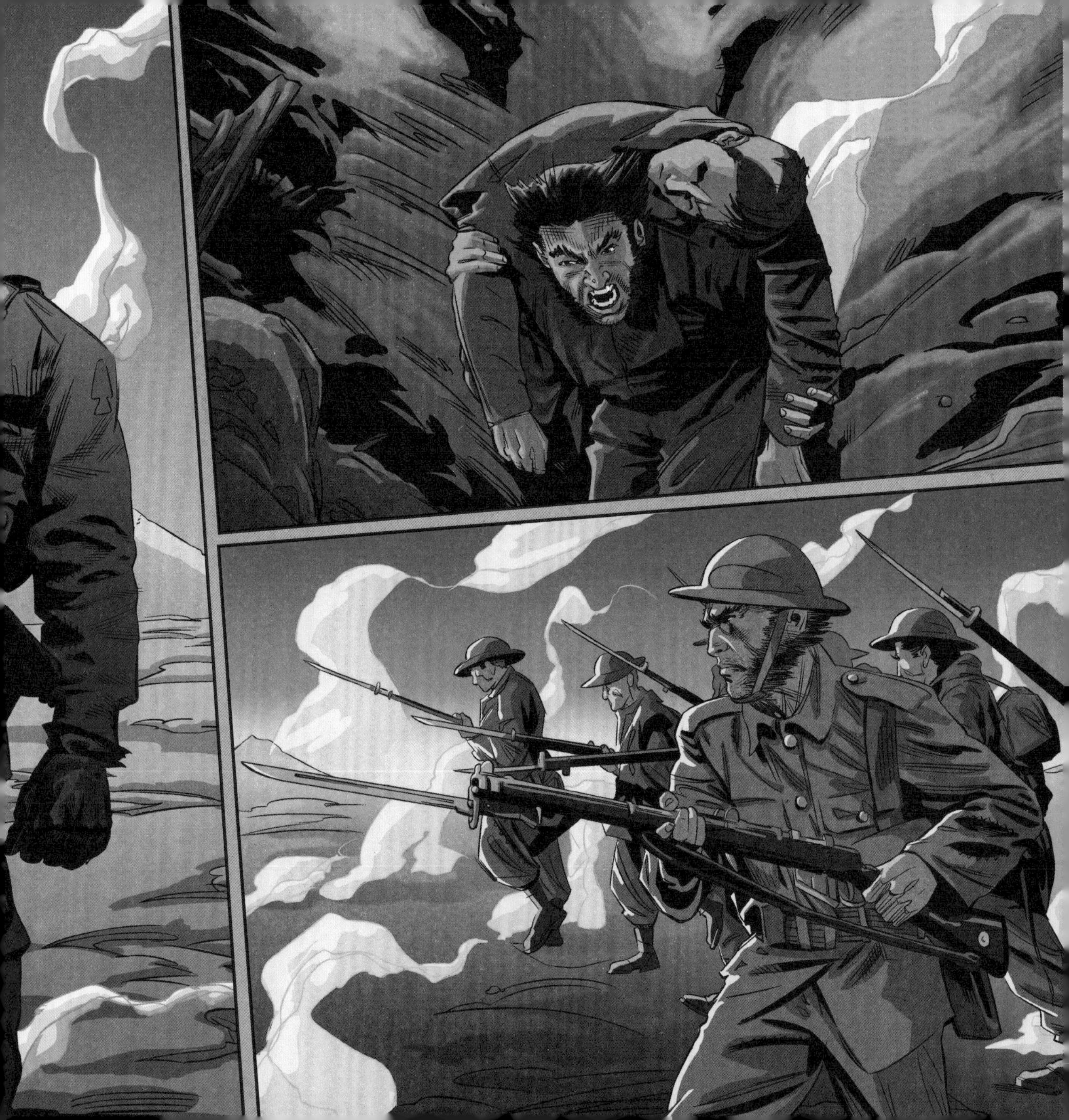

TRAINING & DISCIPLINE

ON ONE OF MY TRIPS TO JAPAN, I trained with a man by the name of Master Ogun. By that point, I was smart enough to figure out that the chip on my shoulder had become too heavy to carry around with me. That Lupine part of me, my heritage as nothing much more than a wild animal, I needed to find a way to keep that down, and traditional martial arts training seemed the only thing that would work.

Tuning your instrument is key. You were born with powers, but there wasn't an instruction manual. You might be able to play chopsticks right out of the gate, but you listen to those who've been there before you, and you're on your way to Carnegie Hall.

Anger and fighting don't mix. I was born with a berserker rage that actually helps in a brawl, but it can also make me go too far. Can't tell you the number of times I brought a situation over its boiling point when I didn't need to. Training taught me to take my time. The idea is to fight smarter than the other guy.

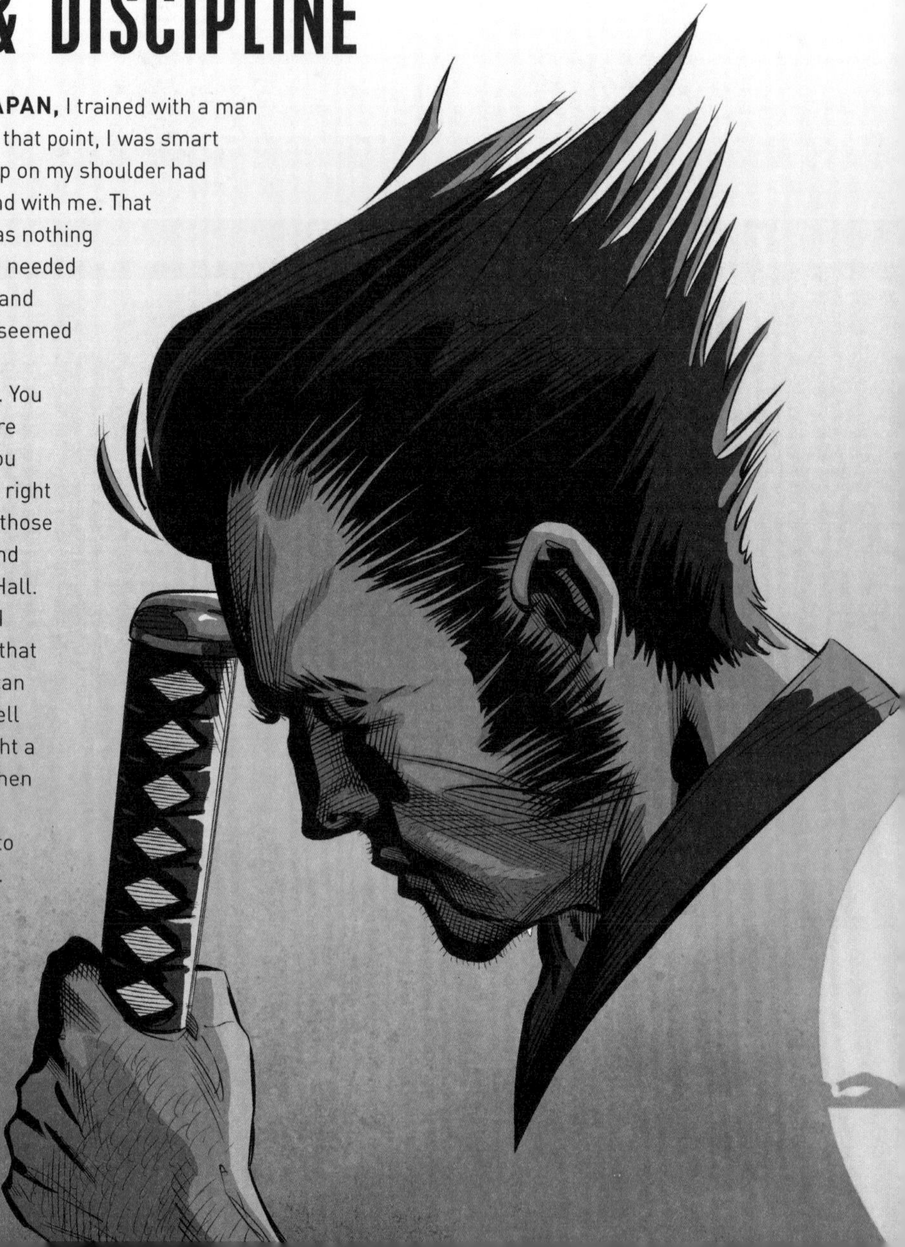

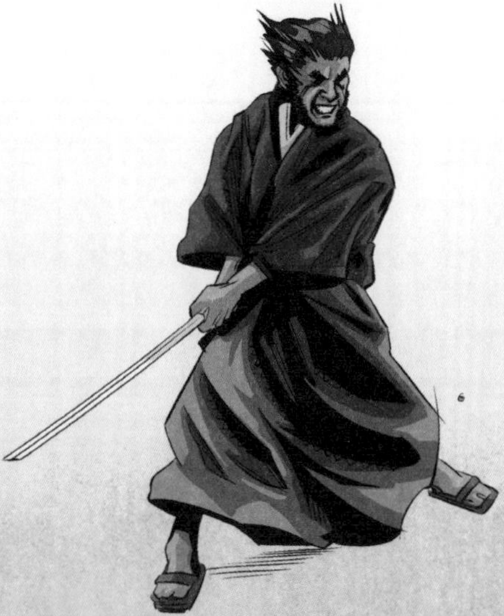

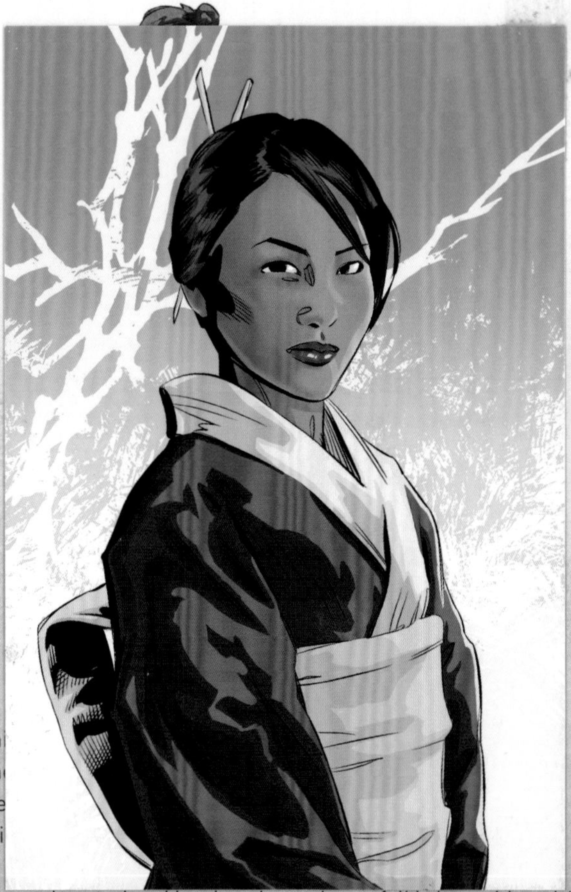

m
m
he
wi

learned control and hard work—and even fell in love with a girl named Itsu. I even had another chance at a life like the one I had with Silver Fox. But Romulus was still watching me and messing with my life, so soon enough Itsu was killed, and I thought the same was true of the child she had inside her belly.

Everything I had learned with my instructors was lost with Itsu, and I let anger guide me for too long after that. My mistake was thinking training ended after the classroom. But the minute you stop learning is the minute you stop being of use to anyone.

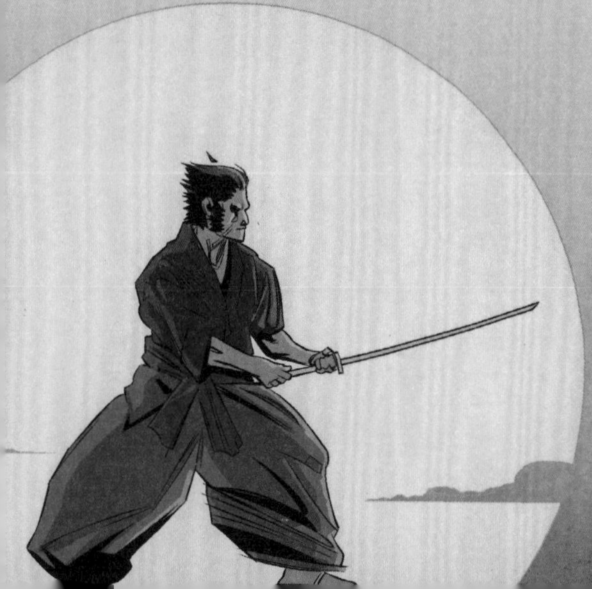

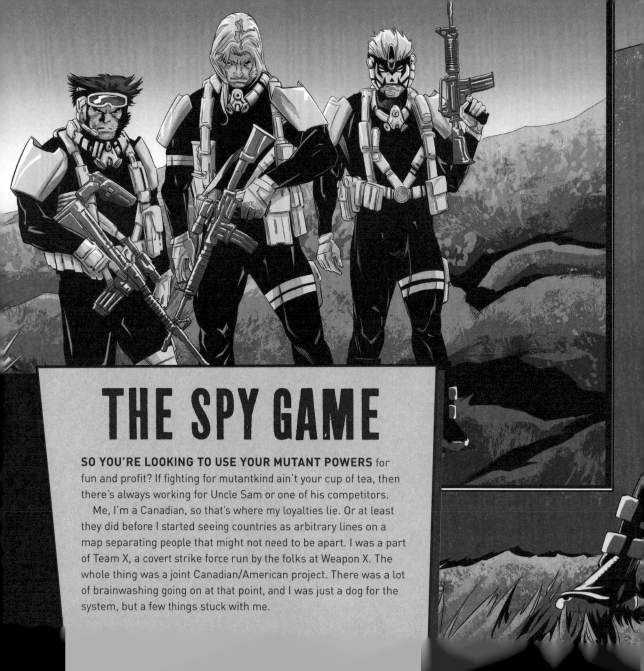

THE SPY GAME

SO YOU'RE LOOKING TO USE YOUR MUTANT POWERS for fun and profit? If fighting for mutantkind ain't your cup of tea, then there's always working for Uncle Sam or one of his competitors.

Me, I'm a Canadian, so that's where my loyalties lie. Or at least they did before I started seeing countries as arbitrary lines on a map separating people that might not need to be apart. I was a part of Team X, a covert strike force run by the folks at Weapon X. The whole thing was a joint Canadian/American project. There was a lot of brainwashing going on at that point, and I was just a dog for the system, but a few things stuck with me.

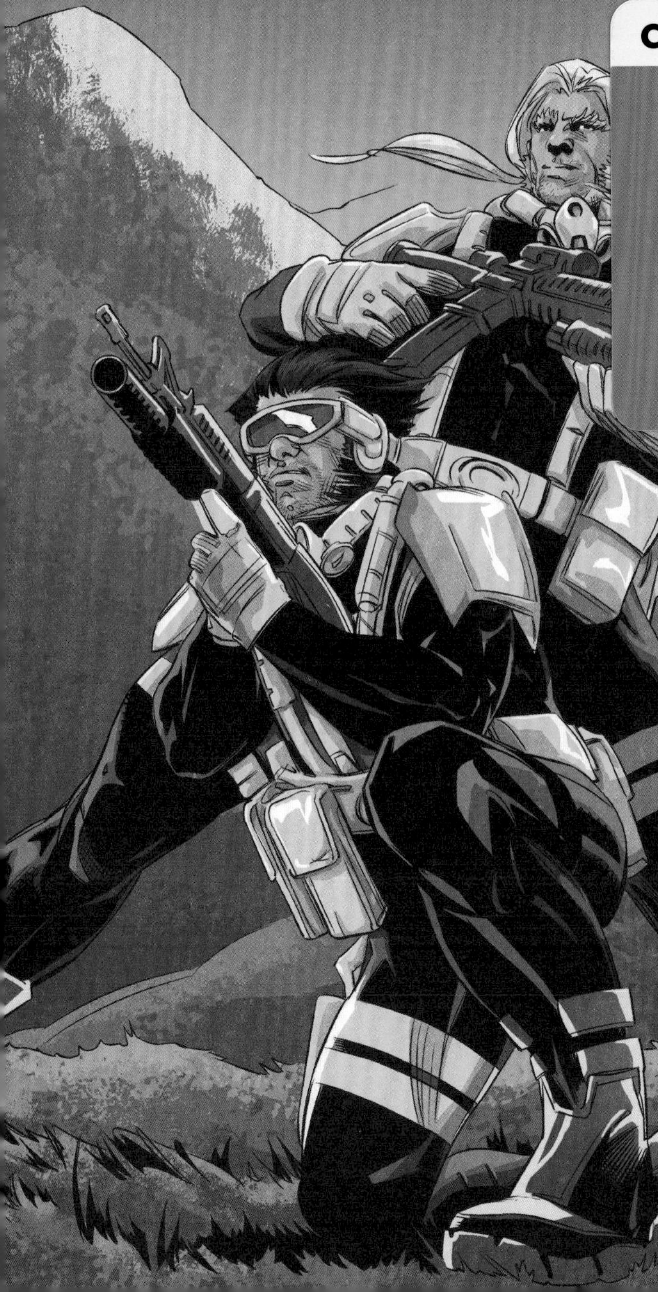

CENTRAL INTELLIGENCE AGENCY

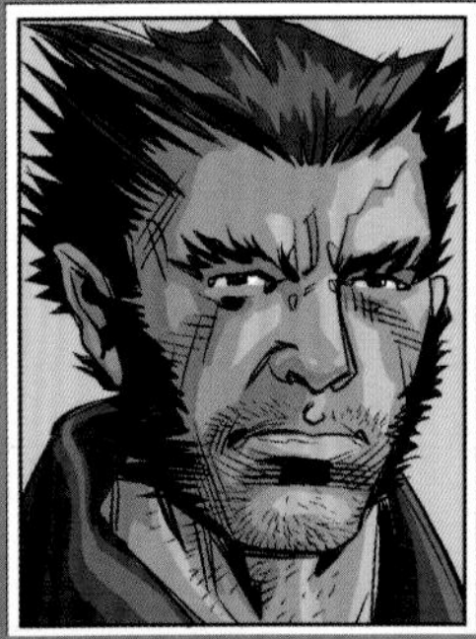

AGENT LOGAN

HEIGHT: 5'3"

WEIGHT: 195 LBS.

EYES: BLACK

HAIR: BLACK

DIRECTOR OF CENTRAL INTELLIGENCE

one to keep quiet about it, either.

Question everything. When I was working for the CIA in Team X, I was partnered with Sabretooth. My brain was so messed up there I was thinking the big guy was my ally. But when he killed a woman named Janice Hollenbeck, I started to remember his true, ugly colors. It shouldn't have gotten to that point. I should have asked more questions.

If you go freelance, know who you're working for. I used to hustle for these guys who were part of an inter-dimensional firm, if you can believe that. Thing called Landau, Luckman and Lake. You don't properly vet your clients, you might end up on the most bizarre trips of your life, traveling to places no man has an honest right to go.

Trust is for another line of work. In a world of double and triple agents, the only voice you listen to when it gets right down to it is the one in your head.

TAKING CONTROL

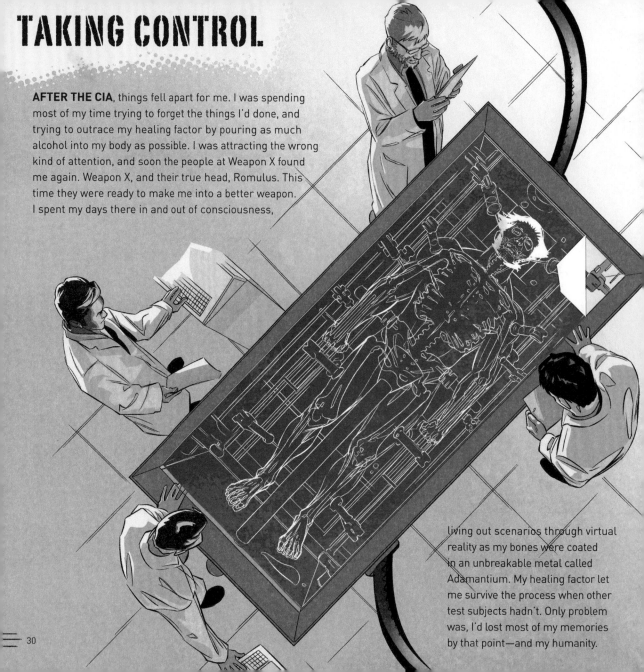

AFTER THE CIA, things fell apart for me. I was spending most of my time trying to forget the things I'd done, and trying to outrace my healing factor by pouring as much alcohol into my body as possible. I was attracting the wrong kind of attention, and soon the people at Weapon X found me again. Weapon X, and their true head, Romulus. This time they were ready to make me into a better weapon. I spent my days there in and out of consciousness, living out scenarios through virtual reality as my bones were coated in an unbreakable metal called Adamantium. My healing factor let me survive the process when other test subjects hadn't. Only problem was, I'd lost most of my memories by that point—and my humanity.

But I got out. I ripped and cut and tore my way out of that place. Went back to the wild to live like an animal. But I'd beaten them. And for the first time in a long time, my life was my own again. I was done being a faithful dog.

When I next found myself, when my mind healed enough to let me head back to civilization, I decided I'd never be a dog again. I'd be something more independent. Something more vicious.

I'D BE A WOLVERINE.

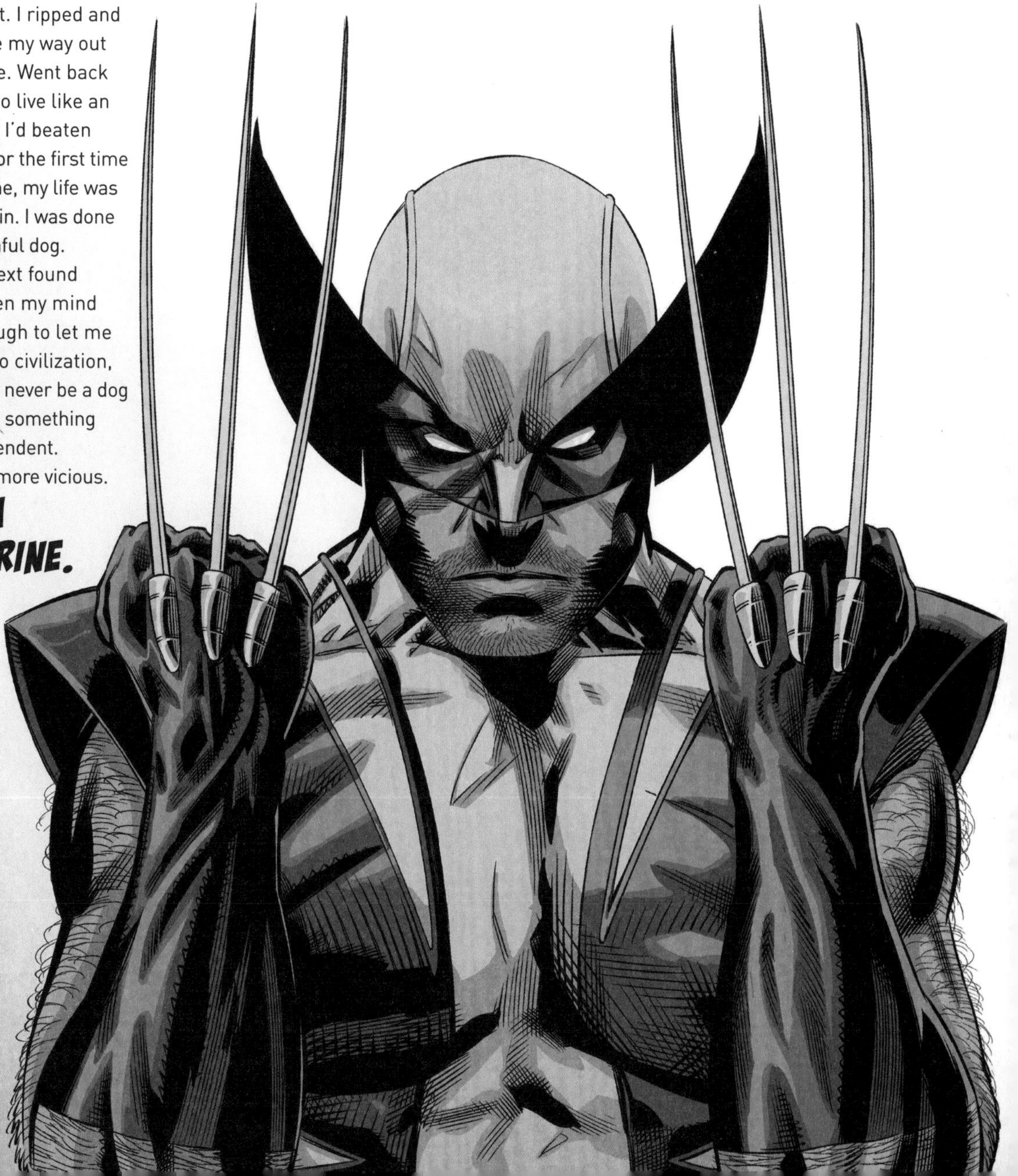

OVERCOMING **WEAKNESS**

THERE'S NOT ONE OF US that doesn't have limitations or an Achilles' heel. It's how you deal with them that defines the kind of mutant you are. Me, I got three big issues. **Carbonadium** is the first. When Adamantium first debuted on the scene, everybody wanted it, and nobody knew how to make it. The Soviets tried, and the result was Carbonadium. Stuff's highly radioactive, but the real trouble for me is it's one of the only things that can negate my healing factor.

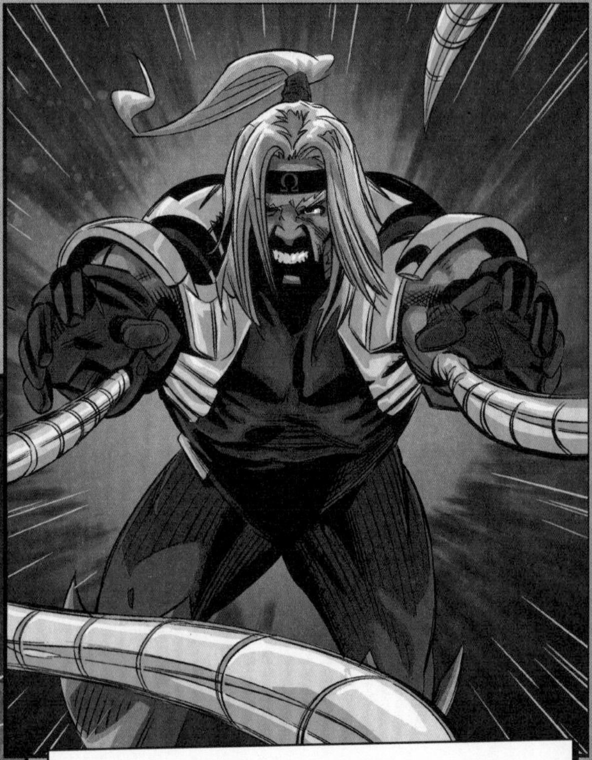

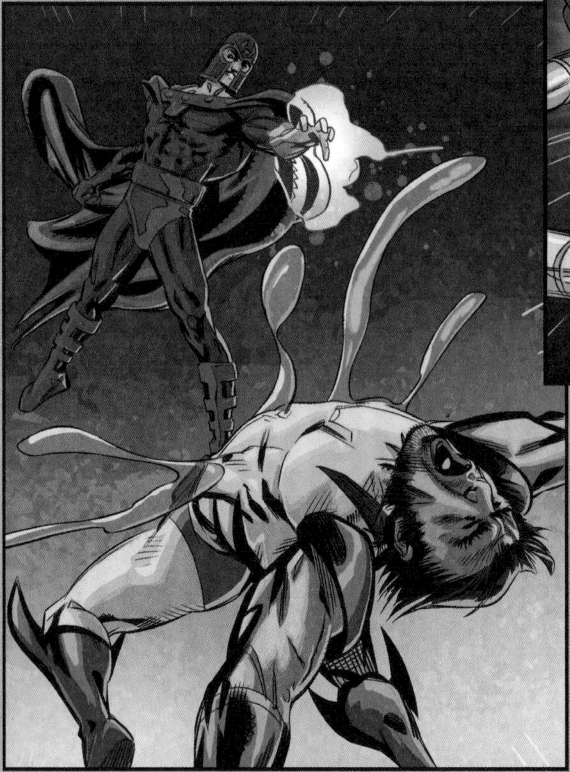

The second is **magnetism**. When every bone in your body is covered with metal, people with magnetic abilities like nobody's favorite mutant, Magneto, become a bigger problem. At one point, the guy ripped the Adamantium right off my bones. With the "help" of another megalomaniac named Apocalypse, I got the metal back, but losing the stuff in the first place was a lesson in pain that I won't forget.

The last one is my own damn fault, a result of shortsighted anger and stupidity. When Itsu was killed back in Jasmine Falls, I left Bando Suboro in favor of a master of the dark arts named Muramasa. This guy took my anger and literally molded it into a weapon, a sword known as the **Muramasa Blade**. It's the only weapon I know of that can cause me permanent damage or kill me if wielded with enough skill. Figure it will prove the end of me someday, but not in the way I originally expected. More on that later.

With all that working against me, I'd be lying if I said I didn't consider giving up and crawling under a rock somewhere. But hiding ain't no way for a man to live, let alone a mutant.

Whatever it is out there that can bring you down, it doesn't matter. You get up every day, you put your pants on, and you go out there and you face it.

It's not about fighting if you know you're gonna win. True test of a mutant is fighting when you know there's no chance in hell you're gonna walk away without some major battle scars.

'Cause in the end, if you got weaknesses, so does the guy you're up against. All you gotta do is find his before he finds yours.

THE SUPER HERO LIFE

I'D MET SUPER HEROES BEFORE. Guys in funny suits like that have been around since World War II. Never thought it'd be my thing, even though I met the criteria as far as powers go.

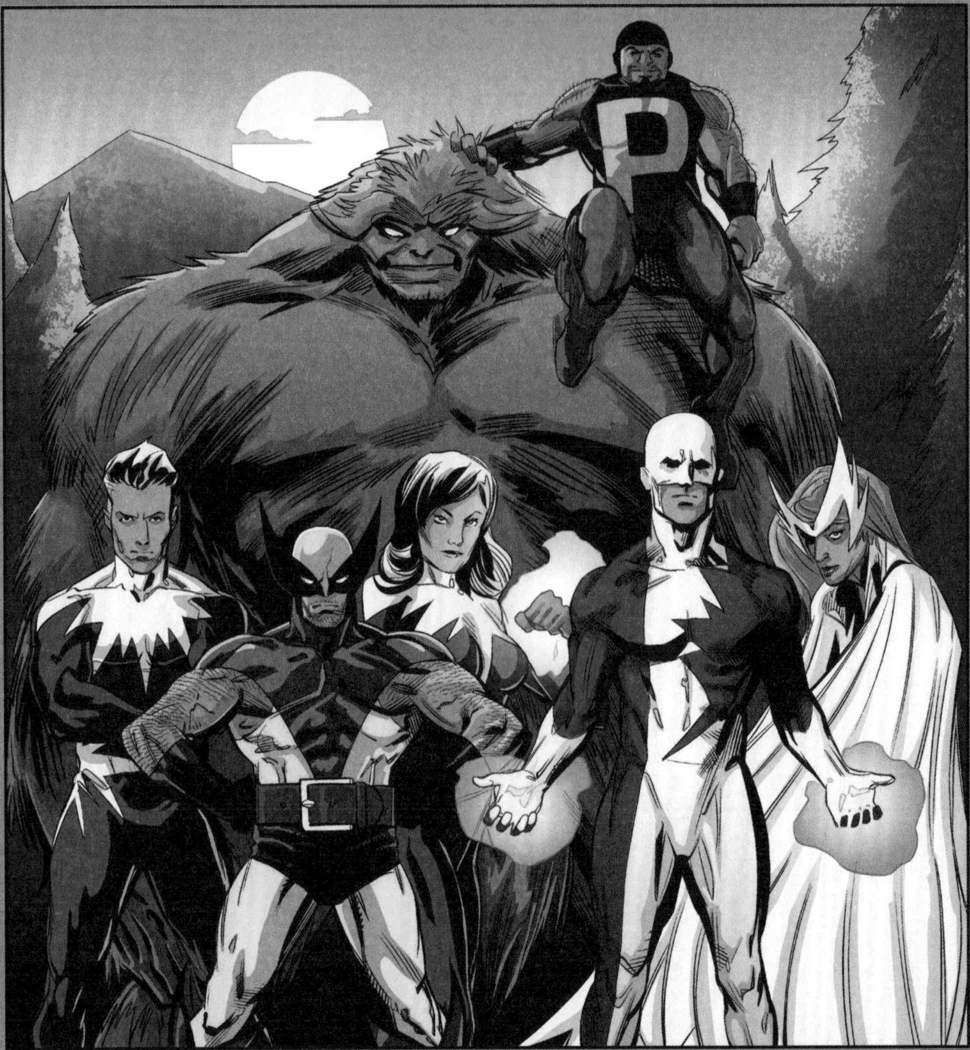

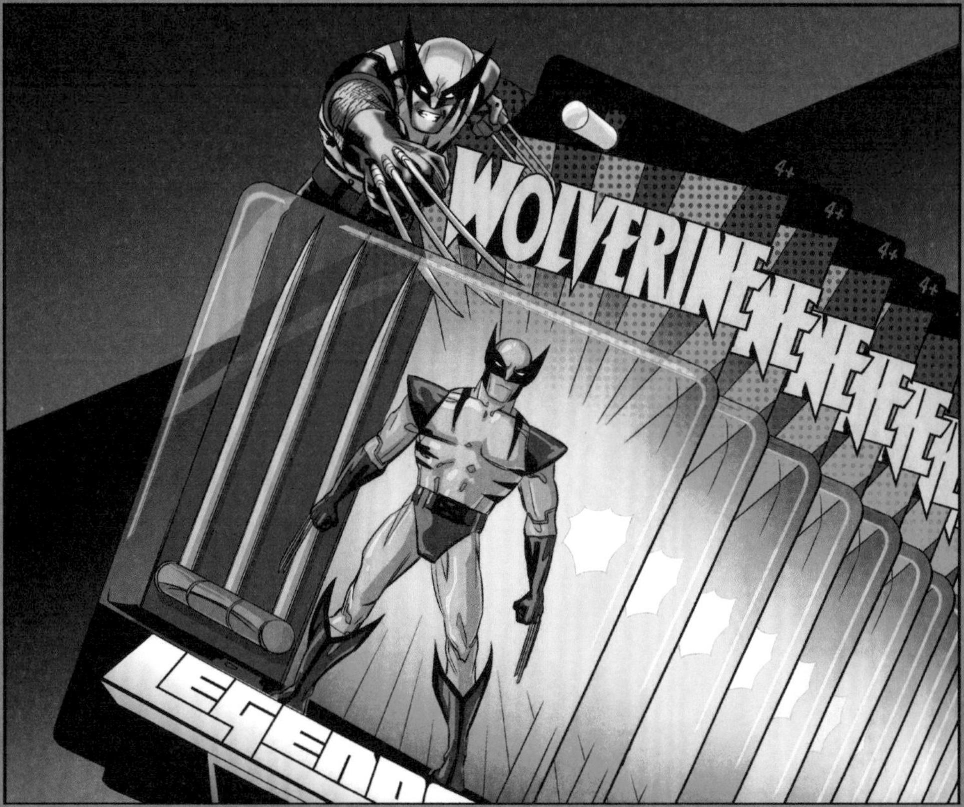
WOLVERINE
4+
4+
4+
4+
LEGEND

But Canada wanted to keep up with the U.S. They wanted their own super people. It was easy work, and like I said, I fit the bill. Pretty soon I was working for the government's Department H, being sent out on covert missions and the like. Even got myself one of those bright costumes to tell the world exactly who I was.

If you go down that road—become a hero—then you gotta be aware of what comes with it. You're any good at the job, people will start to know you. You'll be an instant celebrity. Some people you never met will put you on a pedestal, and others will hate you just for the way you live your life.

But no matter what you do, and I mean no matter what, there's going to be some young mutant out there who sees a bit of himself in you. Whoever that kid is, he's more important than the villain you're fighting or the alien invasion you're holding back. What you do, you do for that kid. And you damn well better think of him when you're on the verge of doing something stupid.

THE COSTUME

NOW HERE'S SOMETHING
I get asked all the time, and frankly, I'm tired of talking about it. Sure I fight "evil mutants" and all that, but why the tights? Why wear a mask if you're not hiding something?

Answer's simple.

It's all about the mindset.

I've got a past, and even if I wasn't aware of the full extent of it when I was just starting out in the hero game, I certainly knew I had hurt more people than I should have or had any right to for that matter. Putting on that mask and the bright colors, it kept me focused.

Becoming Wolverine keeps the berserker rage in check more times than not. It's a reminder that I gotta be a better man than I am.

Simply put, if you wanna act like a hero, look like one.

First look was okay.

Never was a fan of the **whiskers**.

Liked this one a lot more.

Kind of hard to hunt in **bright yellow and blue,** though.

Doesn't really blend in with your surroundings.

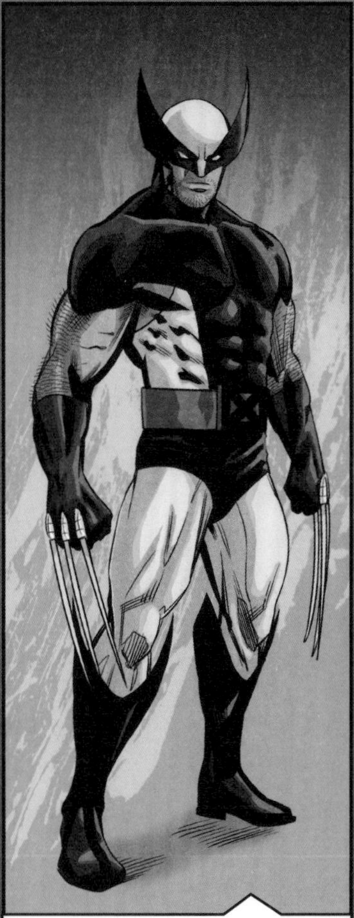

My **personal favorite**.

This one says what I need it to without hitting you over the head with it.

'Cause that's the part I like to do myself.

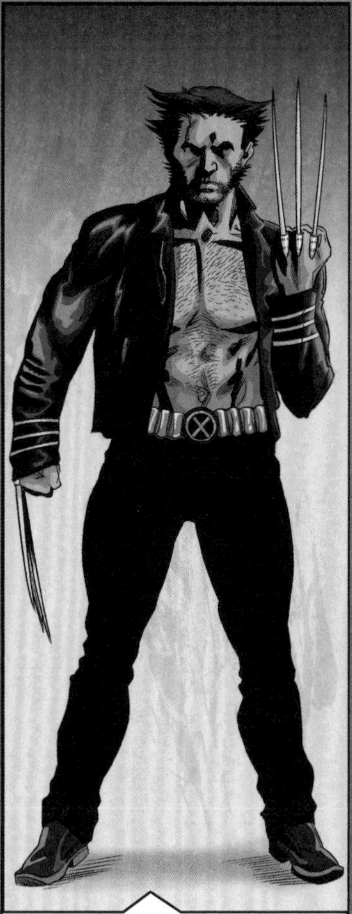

Can't remember whose idea this one was.

But mutants parading around in **matching black leather** uniforms didn't exactly win over the hearts of a suspicious public.

Go figure.

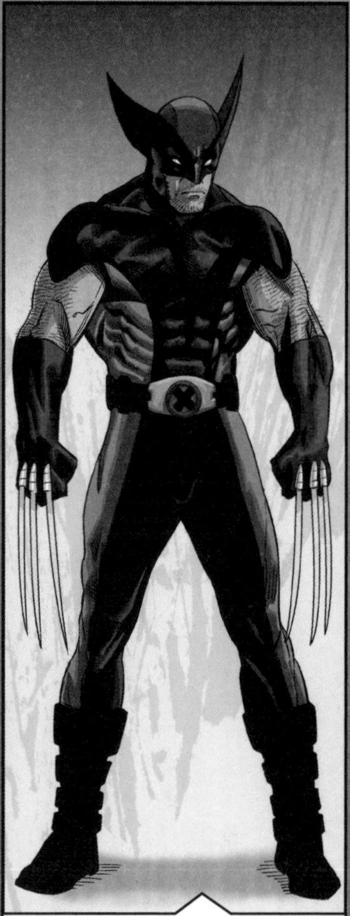

This one is for when I'm doing things for the cause so no one else has to.

Black ops kind of stuff that takes a toll and gets your claws dirty.

Uniform lets me know work has to be done, and the color tells me exactly what kind of work that is.

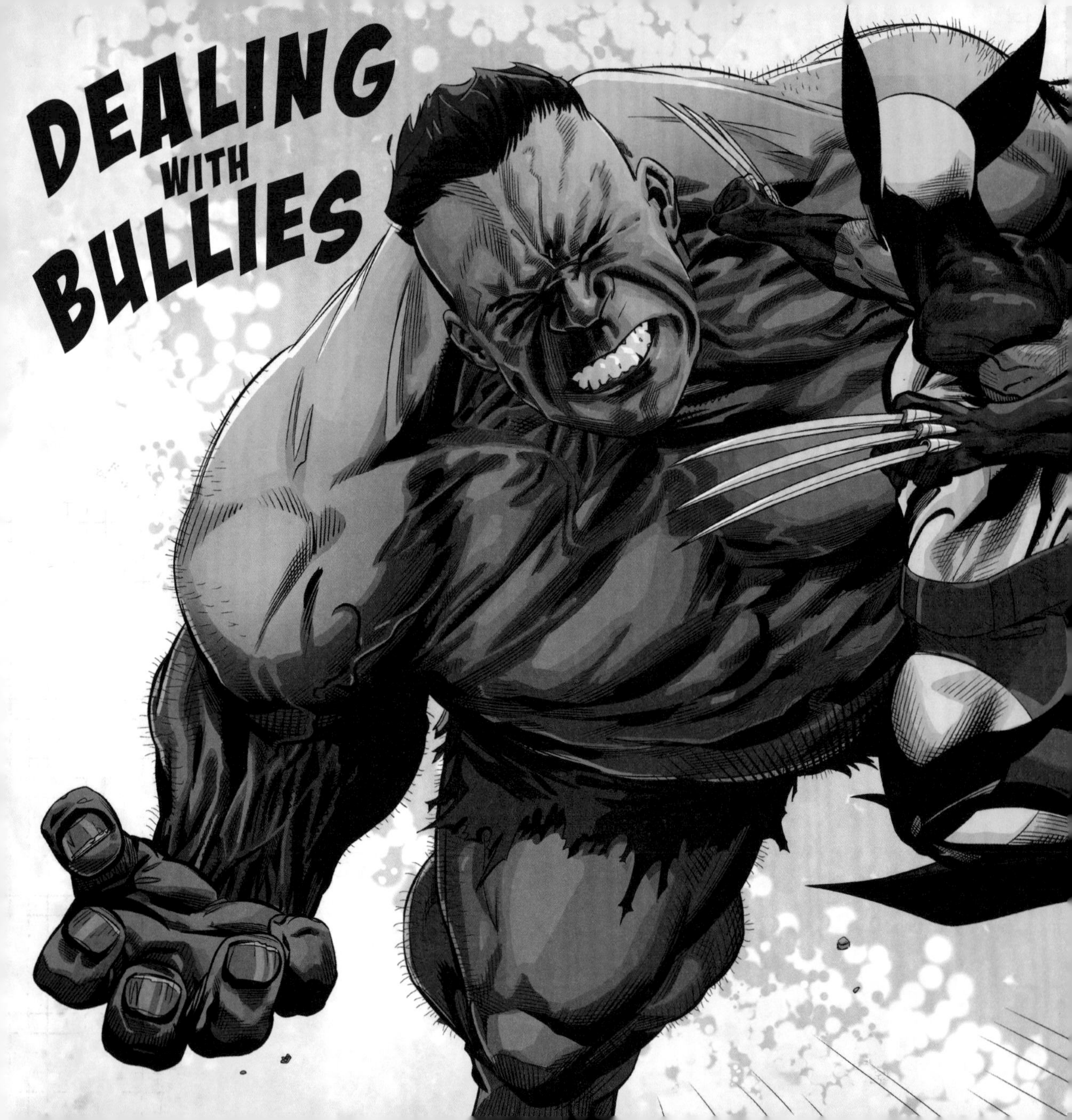
DEALING
WITH
BULLIES

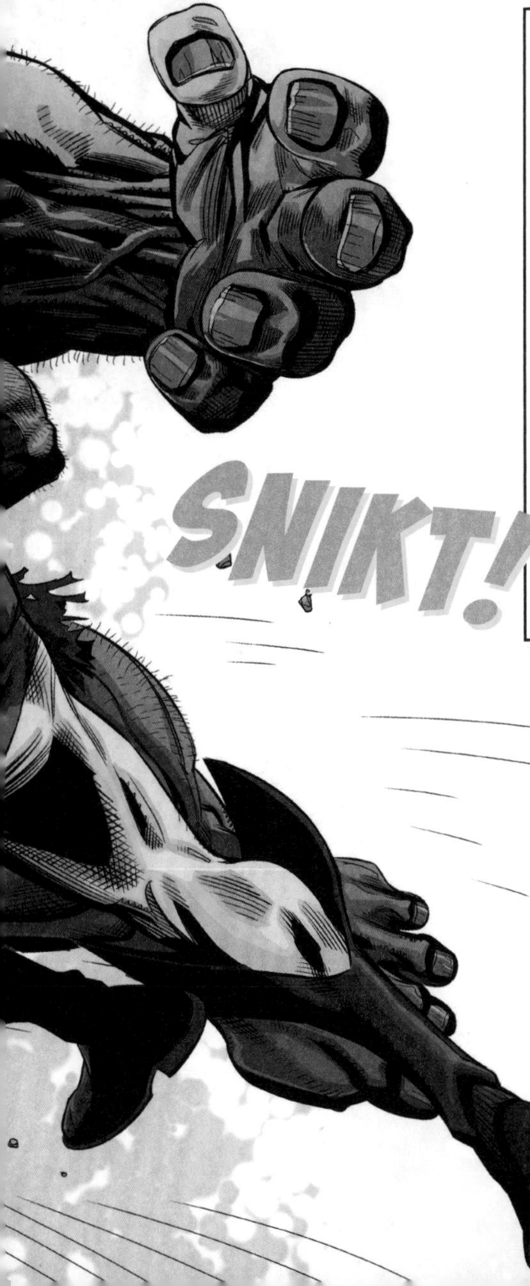
SNIKT!

IT'S JUST A FACT OF LIFE that at one point or another, you're gonna be forced to deal with chumps who get their kicks by pushing you around. I'm a little guy, so I get it more than most. It helps to be able to take a punch or have a body that can heal itself when you can't. But if you're not that lucky, here are a few tips for dealing with the big guys:

Never let them know you're scared. If I'm perfectly honest, I don't get scared a whole lot. Got too much anger in me for that. But I know the feeling, and I know you've already lost the fight if an opponent sees fear in your eyes. Go in ready to enjoy the scrap. The guy you're facing will be able to see that, too. And he won't like it near as much.

One of the first guys I ever had to face as Wolverine was the Hulk. Before our fight, part of me knew I was biting off more than I could chew. Luckily, the rest of me was just curious to see if I could take down the big green guy. Fought him a couple times now. And if you ask me, the refs are still tallying up the points.

Guys like Hulk, they like to toss everybody around, flex their muscles. But deep inside, they're littler than the rest of us. They're overcompensating for something. Maybe daddy didn't love them enough or the It Girl in school wouldn't look them in the eye. If you're lucky or sneaky enough to find out what it is that drives these kinda guys, then you be sure to exploit that. Puts you and Mr. Bigbad on the same playing field.

One thing about bullies is they prey on the weak. So when you're in a fight you started—and this is important, so pay attention—and you know for a fact you can hand the guy his head without much effort, then you gotta look at why you're fighting. 'Cause if you're not fighting the bully, odds are you turned into one yourself.

BEING A TEAM PLAYER

THIS ONE TOOK ME A WHILE TO LEARN. I always understood hunting in a pack, but when things got personal, I liked to do the dirty work myself. Settle my own scores. But there's more to life than hunting, and the more you get out there and do real good, you figure out that you can't do it all by yourself.

I thought I was done with all the brainwashing stuff when I first met the X-Men. But Romulus had plenty of ties to the Canadian military, and it turns out he was still messing with my head and pulling my strings. My last mission for him was to kill Charles Xavier, the head honcho of the X-Men and the guy in charge of the original mutant school. It was the kinda job that was right up my alley.

But Charlie was just as good at head games as Romulus, and pretty soon I found myself joining the X-Men full time. I was still being manipulated, but at least this time it was by the good guys. Charlie was a telepath and saw how shattered my mind had become. So he needed to break it again, like mending a bone that healed wrong the first time around.

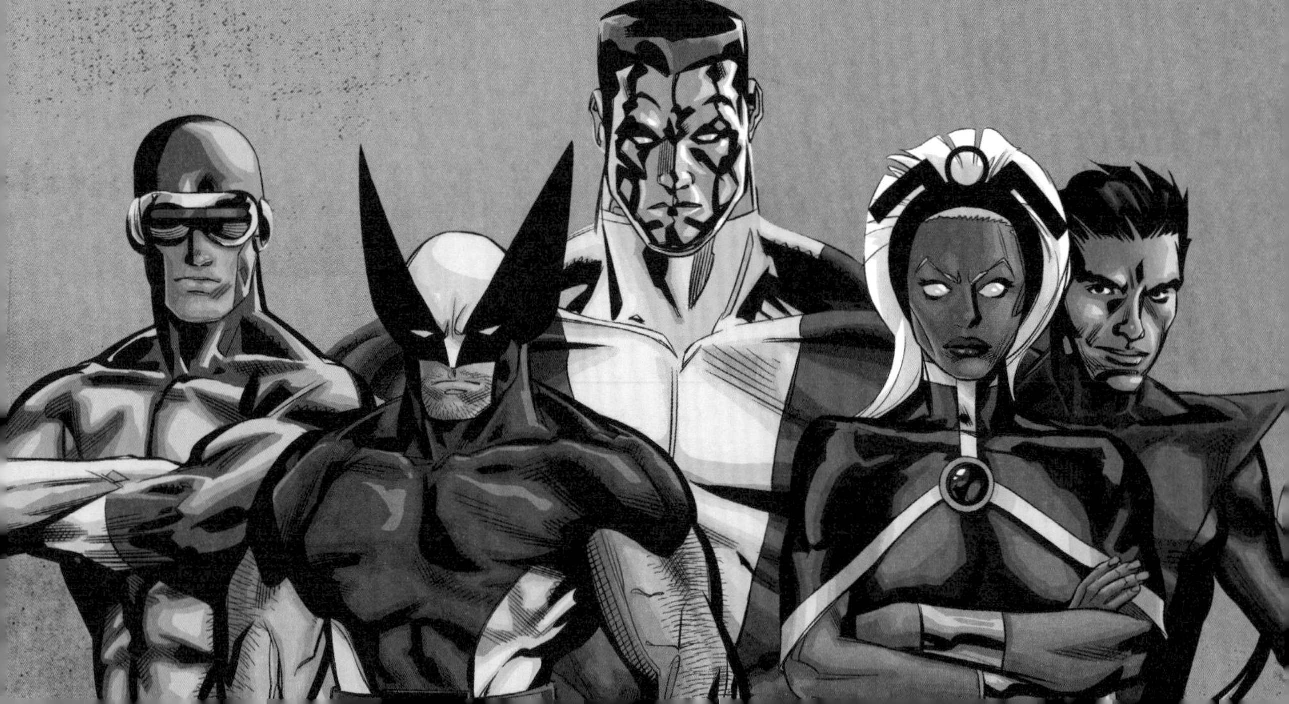

FROM THE DESK OF HEADMASTER CHARLES XAVIER

XAVIER'S SCHOOL FOR GIFTED YOUNGSTERS

Things are progressing with Logan, but not as quickly as I'd hoped. I was certain that he would make a formidable presence on field missions, and I haven't lost any of my faith in him in that regard, but his willingness to work with his teammates varies from individual to individual. While he seems quite comfortable in the company of, say, Jean Grey, for instance, his relationship with Scott Summers leaves much to be desired. Friendly competition is one thing, but there seems to be an animosity lurking beneath the surface that the two are equally guilty of. It is my hope that both Wolverine and Cyclops will someday regard each other as brothers, but that day may never arrive.

Logan's mind is a jagged, unsettling thing. The fact that he is able to even function with so much horror in his past is nothing short of amazing. His mind has been toyed with and altered so many times, he may never remember the extent of his troubled past. And I'm not so sure that's a bad thing.

The simple fact of the matter is that the X-Men need Wolverine. While it is clear he holds a strict moral code, Logan is able to commit acts that would deeply disturb many of the others. While I have no intention of abusing this quality, there may come a time when it becomes a necessity. It is my goal to live in a world where humans and mutants coexist in harmony, but until that day, men like Wolverine are needed to protect those born without his instincts and inner strength.

While he rarely allows therapy sessions, I will continue to do my best to set Logan on the correct path. I trust him to challenge me the entire way, building my resolve and perhaps helping me see the world in a different light.

—Charles Xavier

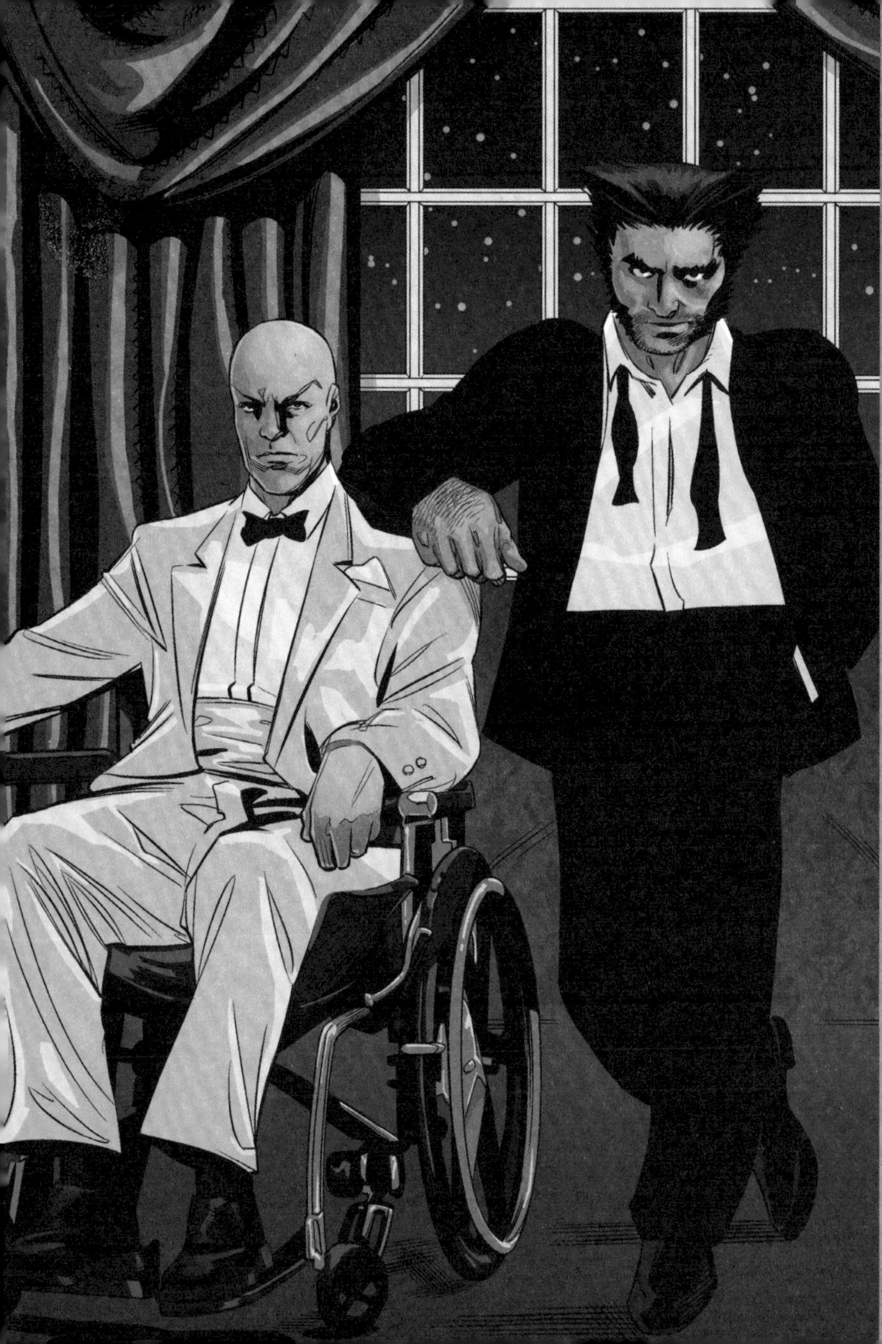

I became an X-Man because I'd been told to be one. I stayed an X-Man because we did good work. But that meant learning to play well with others.

When you're on a team, "me" takes the backseat to "we." So you gotta make sure that everything your team does sits well with you. You find yourself clashing with the big ideas of everybody else too much, and maybe it's time to join up with another group.

There's a lotta pride-swallowing involved. For each mission, you need to see the greater good. You probably think you're the best guy for every assignment, but that ain't the case. You don't send Iceman to the Sahara. And you don't send Wolverine into a business negotiation. Know the kind of weapon you are, and know when to keep your finger off the trigger.

Think with your head, not with your heart. When you're in the field, it's not your job to worry about your pals or your girlfriend. You watch each other's backs, sure, but you get the job done and trust your equals to be just that.

MAKING FRIENDS

I'M PROBABLY NOT THE GUY to be writing this part. Seems more like something that Jubilee or Kitty Pryde should tackle. Still, I somehow managed to make plenty of friends during my time in the X-Men, so I guess I'm not the worst choice. While I'm not one to bring it up much if I can avoid it, I'm glad I've let my guard down enough to let some of these people in.

Know who has your back. Know their powers in and out. Know their weaknesses. Know what they can do that you can't. If you become friends because of that, that's fine. If you don't make an effort to know people, you're not going to last long in any kinda job.

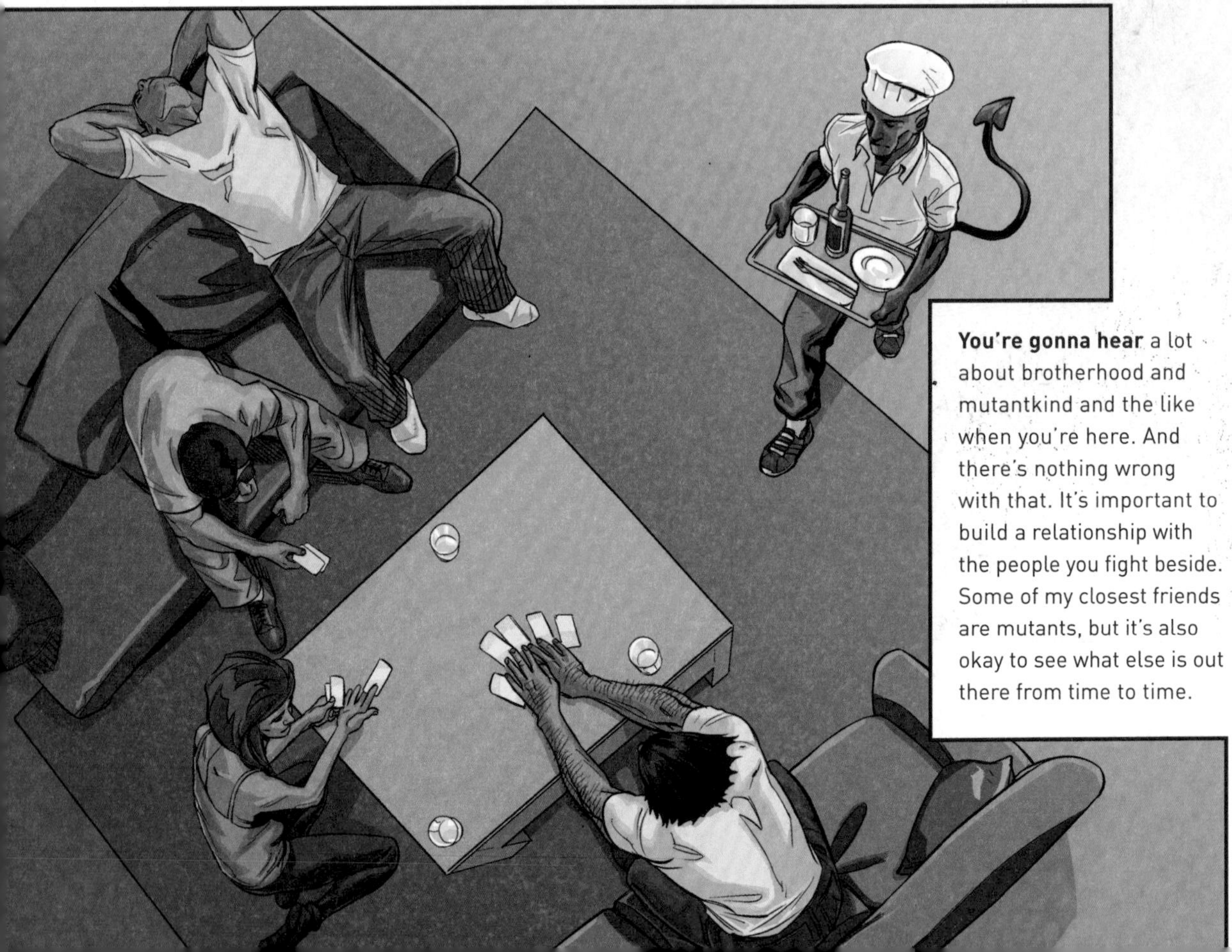

You're gonna hear a lot about brotherhood and mutantkind and the like when you're here. And there's nothing wrong with that. It's important to build a relationship with the people you fight beside. Some of my closest friends are mutants, but it's also okay to see what else is out there from time to time.

Make an effort to meet those different than you. The guys you butt heads with could know a way out of a tough situation that you'd never think up yourself. Every group needs a few people with a stick up their butt. But feel free to mess with them now and again. Back in our heyday, I don't think a week passed when I wasn't making some part of Cyclops' life miserable. To be fair, he did the same to me every chance he got. And believe it or not, we both came out a little better for it.

Take some time off now and again. Bonding can help teamwork, but besides that, you just need to give the hero thing a rest every once in a while. Doesn't matter if your company's a brimstone-smelling little elf or a Cajun who's constantly looking behind you to scope out the women at the bar.

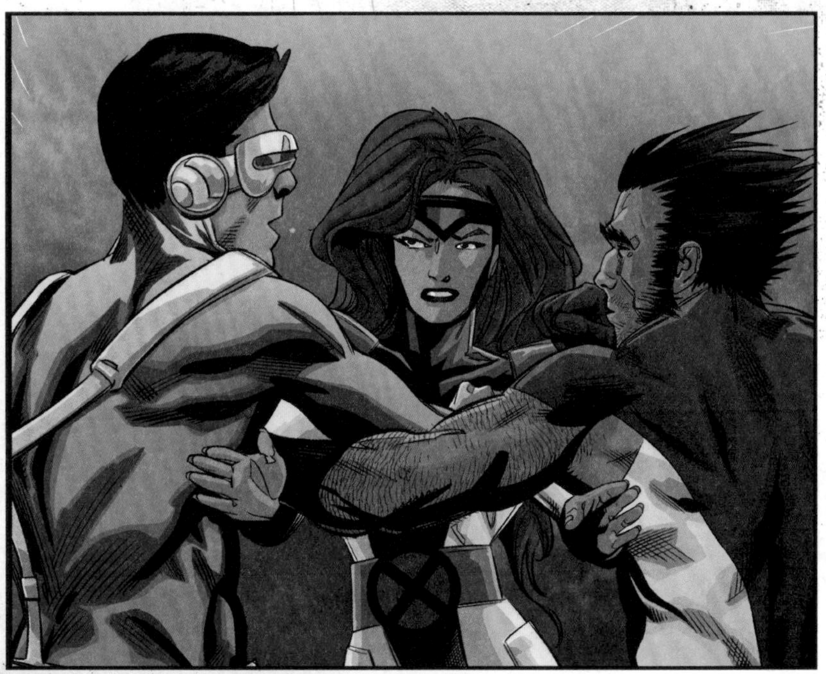

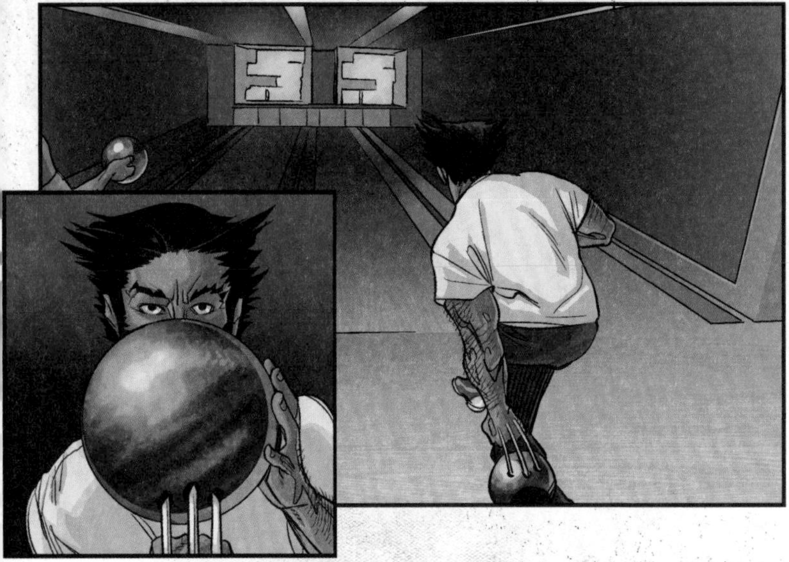

You might like your alone time, but there ain't nothing that's gonna help you more than hanging up the tights and forgetting it all for a bit.

All that said, don't let everybody in. Not everyone is destined to be your "bestest pal." Exercise caution and never drop your guard completely. Life for a mutant isn't the same as life for everybody else. We got enemies just by existing. Anybody can turn on you at any time. But if you know your friends, in most cases, you'll be able to sniff that sort of thing out way ahead of time.

MAKING ENEMIES

NOW THIS PART comes naturally for me. But you don't need my advice on how to make people hate you. And frankly, I wish I wasn't as good at it as I am. But what I can tell you about is some types from my own past that you might wanna steer clear of. And if you can't, here's some thoughts on how to take them down.

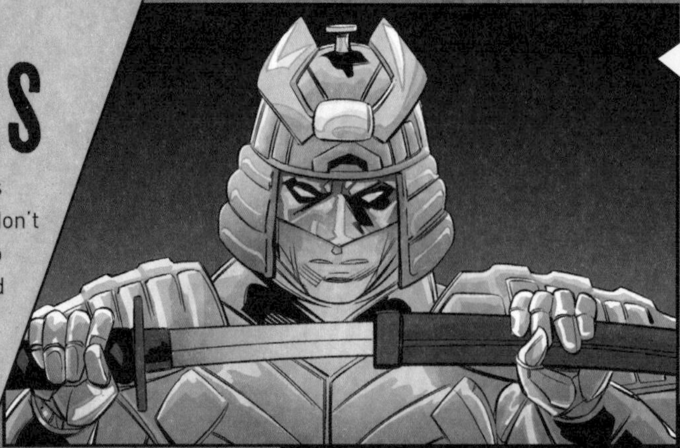

SILVER SAMURAI

Silver Samurai's good at what he does. Good, not great. He's got a code of honor, and to get to him, all you gotta do is have him breach that code, then point out exactly what he's done.

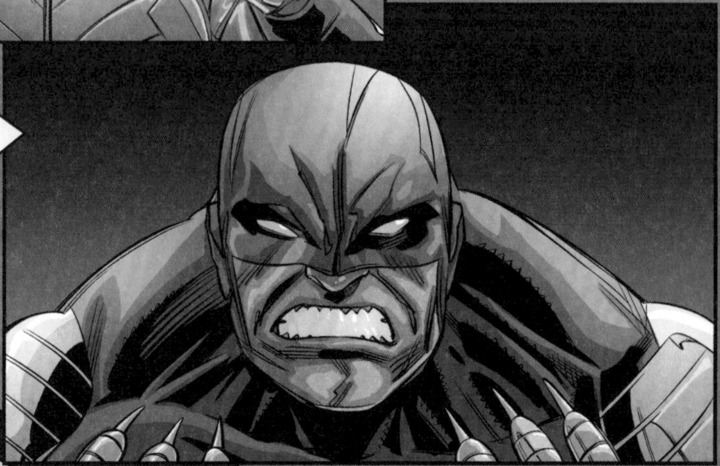

CYBER

Me and Cyber go back a long ways. Guy's got Adamantium armor and poison in his fingertips. Don't mean the rest of him ain't riddled with weak spots, though.

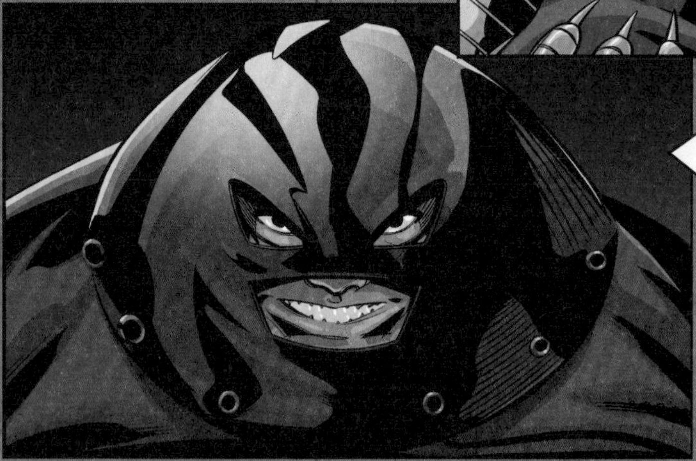

JUGGERNAUT

Juggernaut's almost on Hulk's level when it comes to brute strength. If you want to get anywhere with this guy, you gotta get rid of that helmet. Pry that sucker off, and then let the telepaths do what they do best.

LADY DEATHSTRIKE

Lady Deathstrike's got blinders on when she comes into a fight. She thinks her father's past experimentation with Adamantium gives her ownership of the stuff. Play into that anger, and you're already halfway to a win.

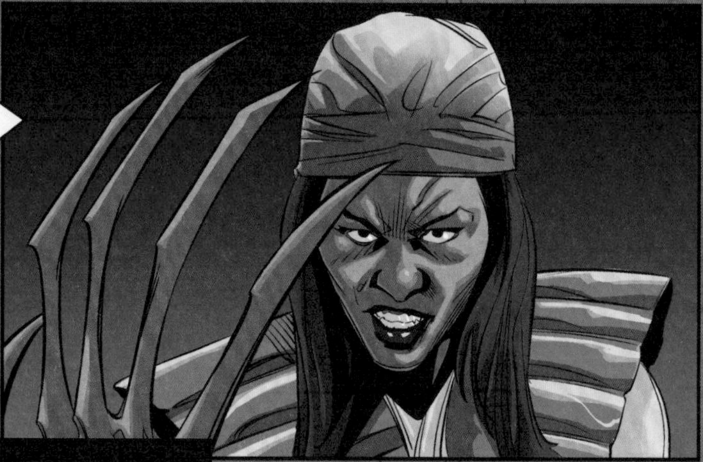

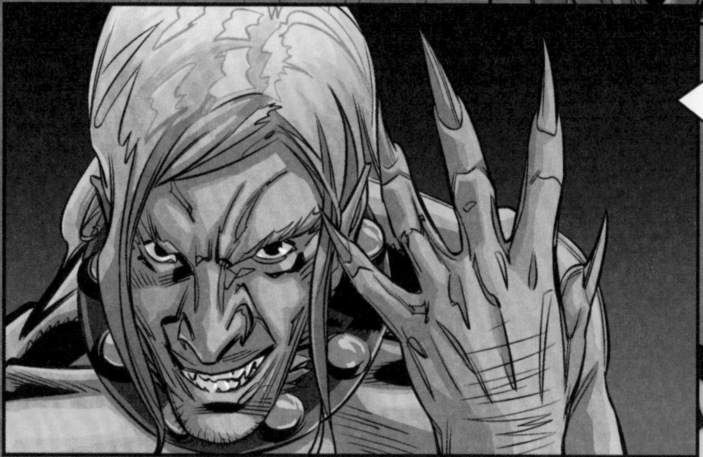

WILD CHILD

Wild Child likes to think of himself as the second coming of Sabretooth. More like the diet version, you ask me. He might be just as savage, but he ain't got none of the grit to really pose a threat.

MAGNETO

This guy controls magnetic fields. Not the type you want to go against if you can't even look at a metal detector without setting the thing off. If I knew an easy way to take him down, I would have done it years ago. Fact is, Magneto only loses when deep down he wants you to win.

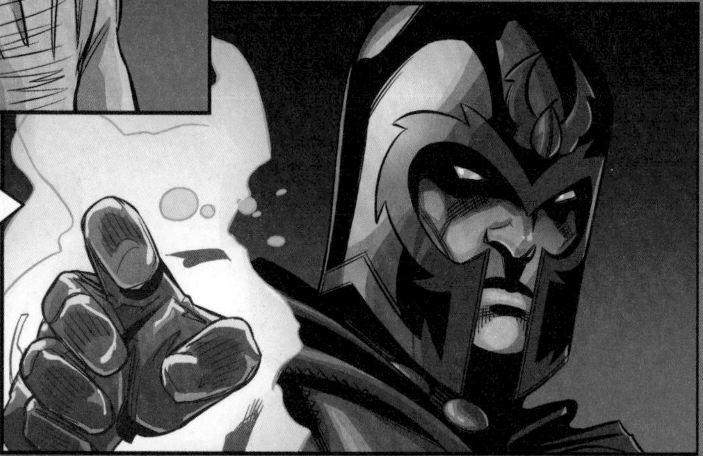

USING WHAT YOU *HAVE*

YOU'VE HEARD PEOPLE TELL YOU to "just be yourself." Heard that your whole life, I'd guess. Well, there's nothing wrong with that advice. It's the only way to get the results you really want—on and off the battlefield.

You got people like **Storm or Cyclops**. They're not about close-in fighting. They're about zapping the bad guy from across the room and never letting him get close enough to do anything about it. But I ain't got that advantage.

Take me, for instance. I'm not a long-distance guy. I'm short, and even though I'm quick, there's plenty that can get from here to there faster than me. I'm aware of who I am, and knowing that gets me through every scrap I get into.

A lot of folks, they go buy their meat at the supermarket and never have to even see the cow they're about to eat. I'm the kind of guy that likes to look his food right in the face. So **close-quarters fighting**'s for me, even if I did have a choice in it. To me, there's something not right about putting a bullet in a man from the safety of a nearby rooftop. If I'm taking you down, you're gonna know it's me who's doing it.

Close-in fighting means getting dirty, but it's a good equalizer. Mutants able to shoot projectiles or some moron with a gun that makes him feel like he's a super-soldier—they're pretty much helpless if they let you get in their personal space. Even if long distance is your thing, you can't skimp on the close combat training. That's the stuff that's going to save your life.

The opposite applies, too. If you're a close-quarters guy, you don't want to be a sitting duck when there's distance between you and your enemy. Find a way to get where you need to be, as quickly as you can, whether that's through stealth or something more unconventional.

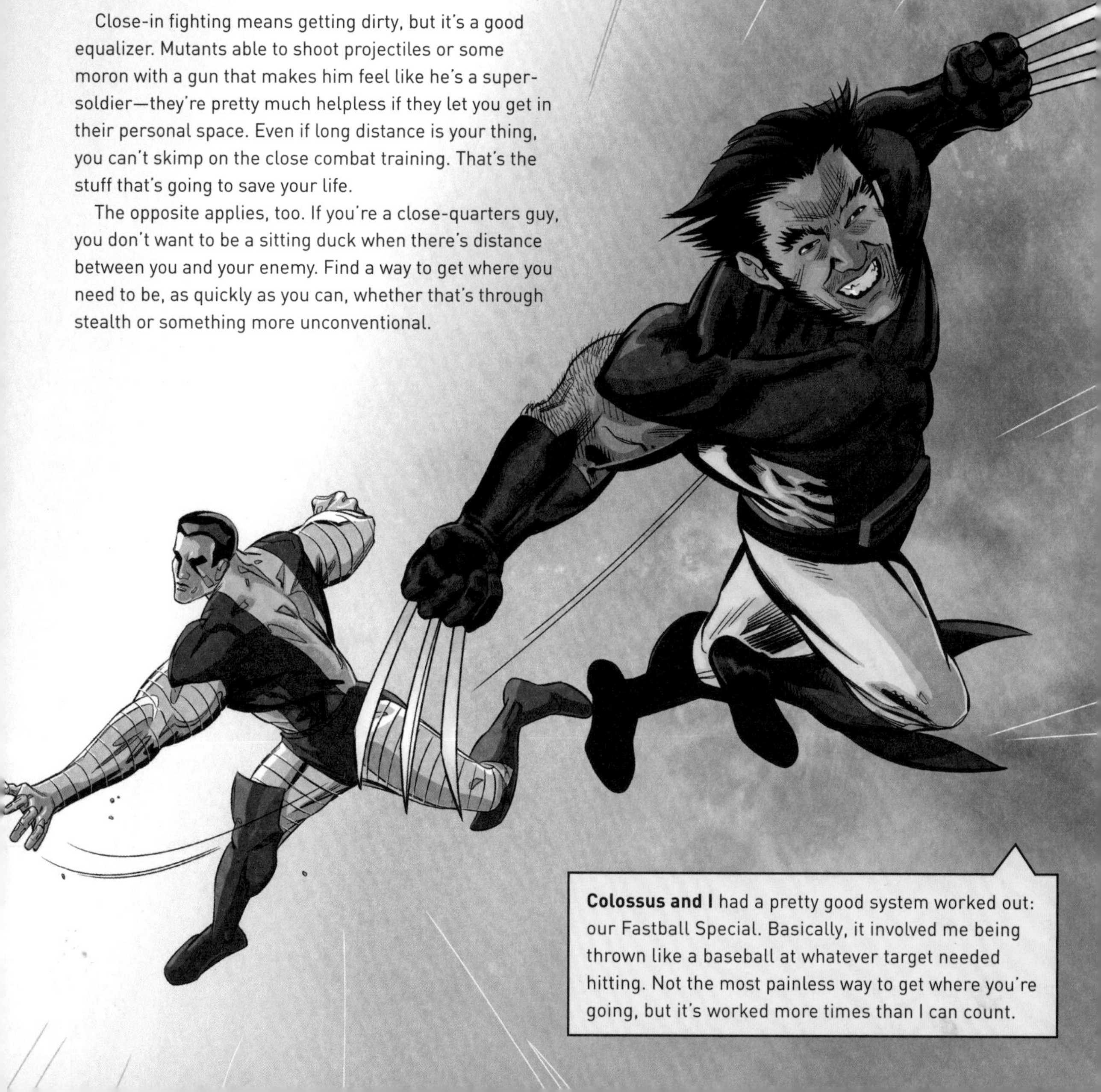

Colossus and I had a pretty good system worked out: our Fastball Special. Basically, it involved me being thrown like a baseball at whatever target needed hitting. Not the most painless way to get where you're going, but it's worked more times than I can count.

LYING LOW

AS A MUTANT, you already know the importance of staying out of the spotlight from time to time. Besides the annoying super-fans, you gotta worry about the so-called "Super Villains" looking to make a name for themselves by putting a fight with you on their résumé. Even I'm not always in the mood for a scrap, so here are some tips to keeping your private life private.

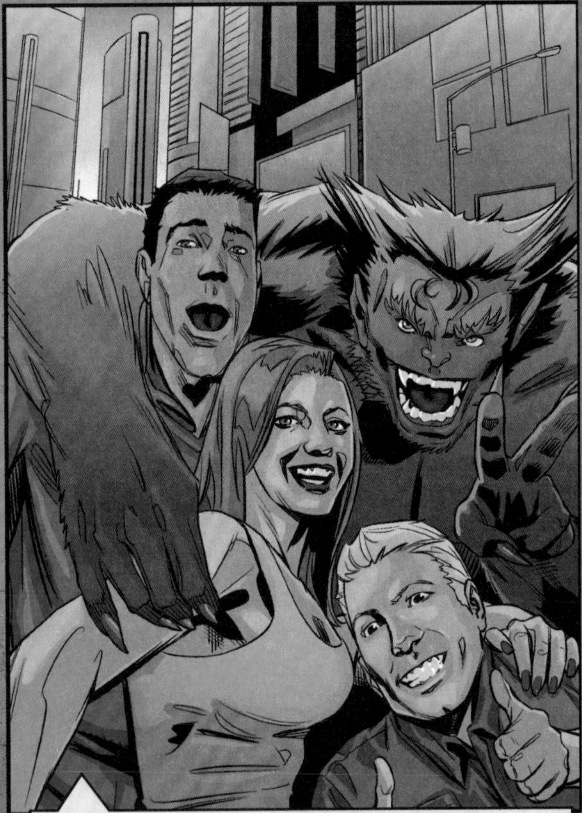

Don't parade around in your uniform. The costume's not for bar hopping or taking an evening jog. Work clothes are for work.

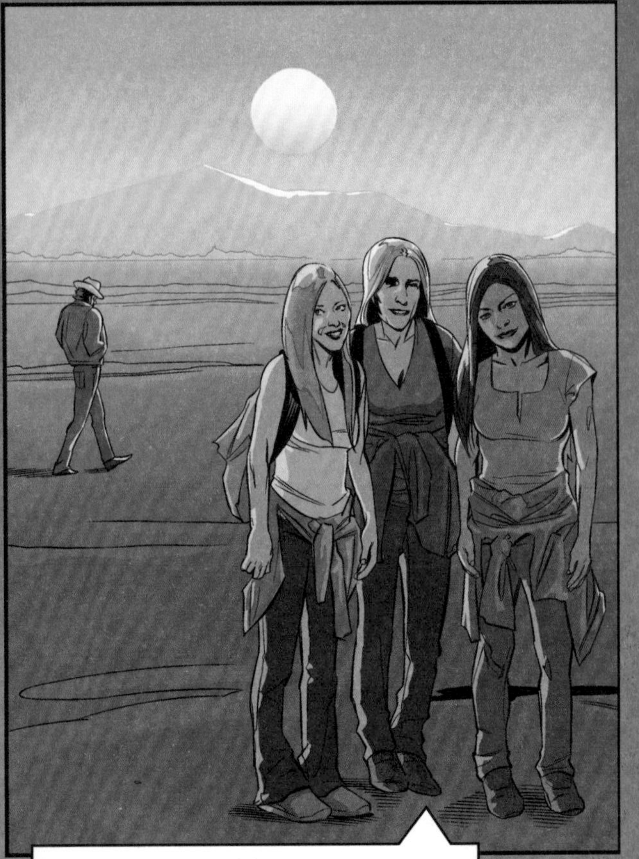

There was a time with the X-Men when **everybody thought we were dead**. And let me tell you, I never felt so free in my life. If people ain't looking for you, half the time, they don't even notice you when you're standing right in front of their face. You get an opportunity like that, don't pass it up.

Try not to use your powers on the sly. You may think you're being sneaky about it, but every place has cameras these days. One minute you're freezing some guy's beer with your ice powers or whatever you got, and the next a team of anti-mutant extremists are chasing you down a dark alley after watching a cell phone video of the whole thing. You don't need to hide being a mutant, but the second you start proving "them" right by using your powers to cause trouble, then you start hurting all of us.

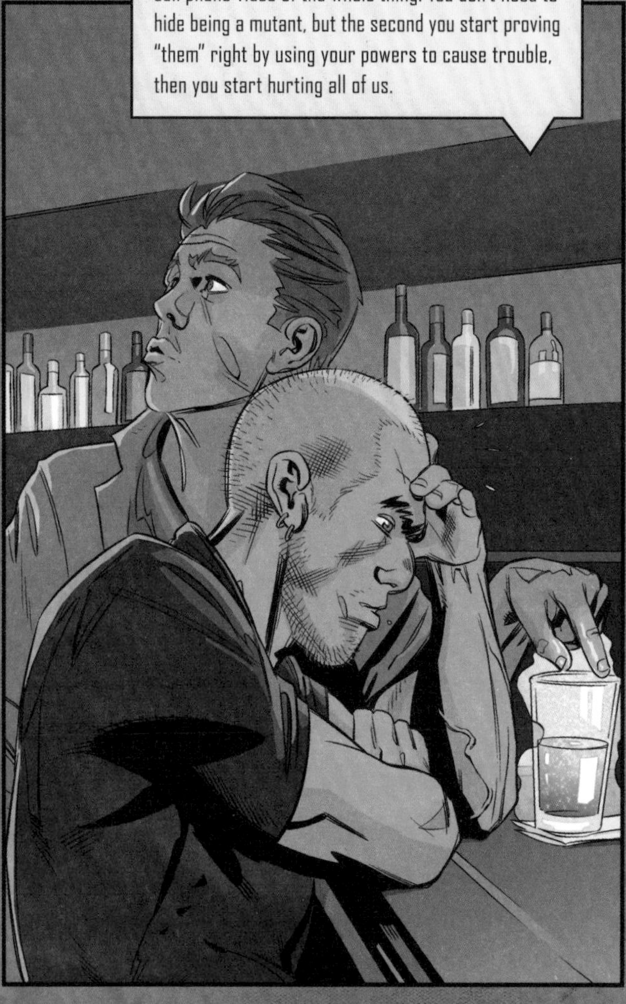

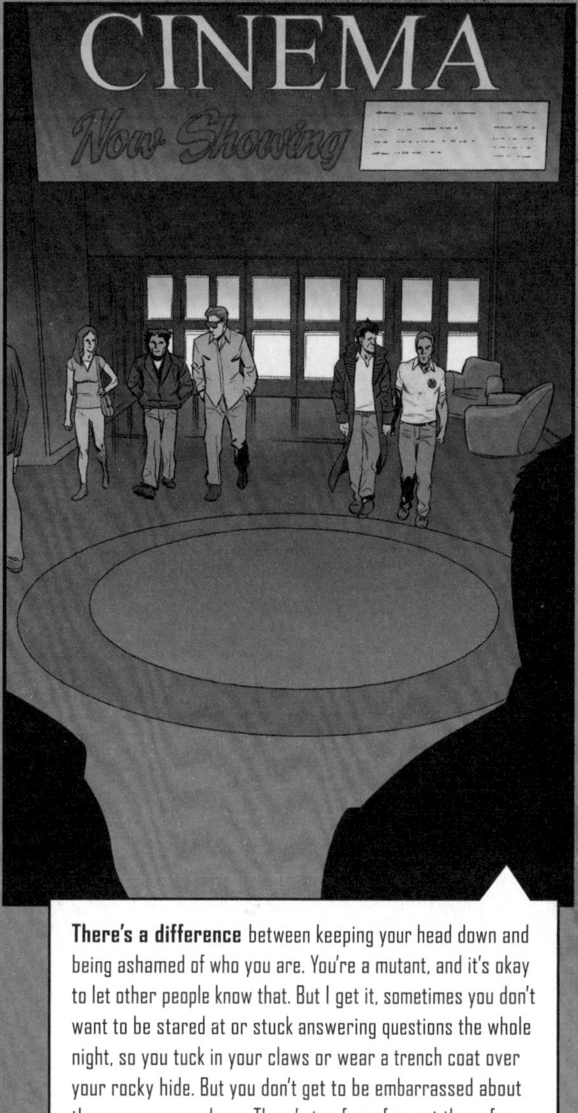
CINEMA
Now Showing

There's a difference between keeping your head down and being ashamed of who you are. You're a mutant, and it's okay to let other people know that. But I get it, sometimes you don't want to be stared at or stuck answering questions the whole night, so you tuck in your claws or wear a trench coat over your rocky hide. But you don't get to be embarrassed about the way you were born. There's too few of us out there for that kind of nonsense. You got a right to privacy, but you got an obligation to be who you are.

CHOOSING THE **RIGHT PARTNER**

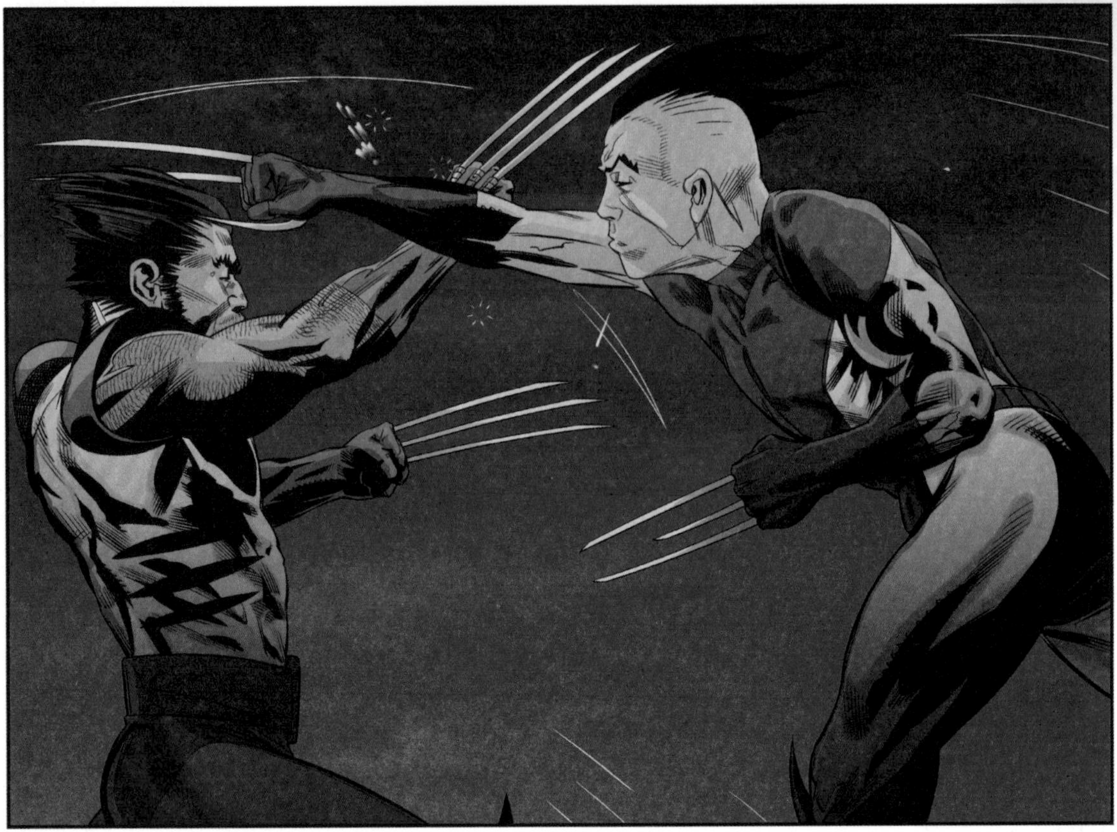

I'VE HAD THE PRIVILEGE TO FIGHT beside a lot of good men and women in my day. Fought beside plenty of the worst kind of folks, too. When it comes to picking a partner, you gotta make sure you know how to tell the difference.

In real life, I've never been any good about being a dad. You probably heard about my boy, Daken. Long story short, I thought he'd been killed when his mother, Itsu, was murdered. Instead, he grew up hating me, thanks to the work of Romulus. And when given the chance, I couldn't undo that kind of damage. I don't know. Maybe I didn't try hard enough.

Even with that kind of terrible record, in the Super Hero world, people keep looking at me as some sort of father figure. I've been a mentor to some kids I couldn't be prouder of.

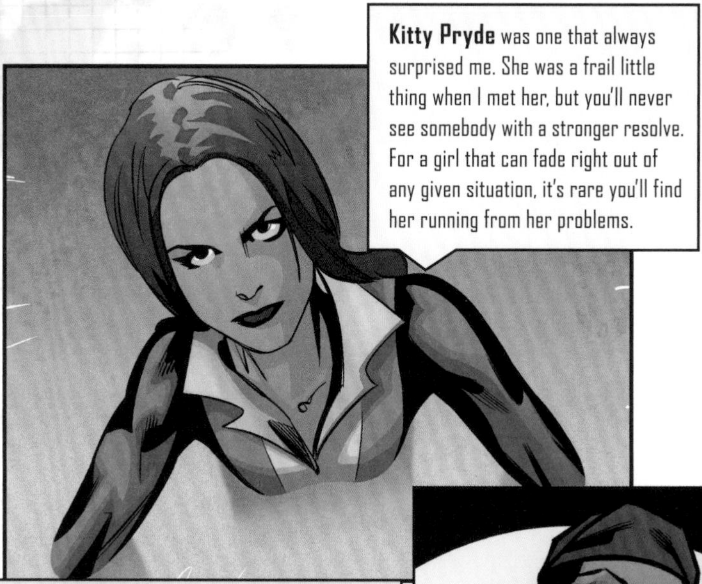
Kitty Pryde was one that always surprised me. She was a frail little thing when I met her, but you'll never see somebody with a stronger resolve. For a girl that can fade right out of any given situation, it's rare you'll find her running from her problems.

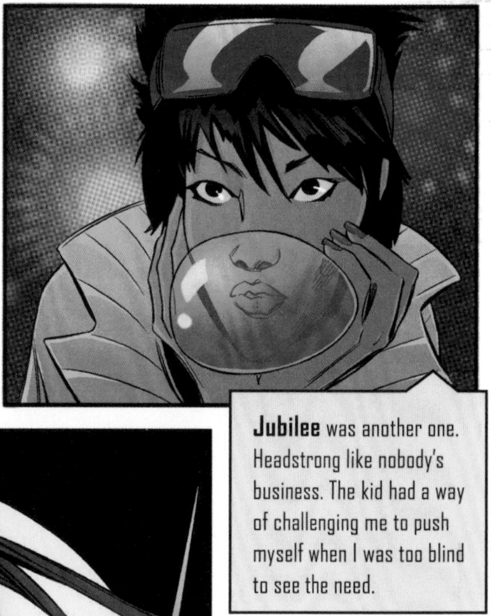
Jubilee was another one. Headstrong like nobody's business. The kid had a way of challenging me to push myself when I was too blind to see the need.

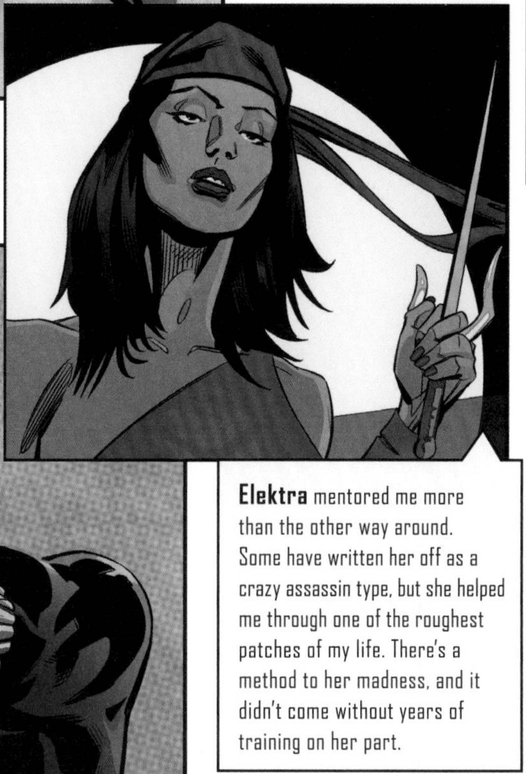
Elektra mentored me more than the other way around. Some have written her off as a crazy assassin type, but she helped me through one of the roughest patches of my life. There's a method to her madness, and it didn't come without years of training on her part.

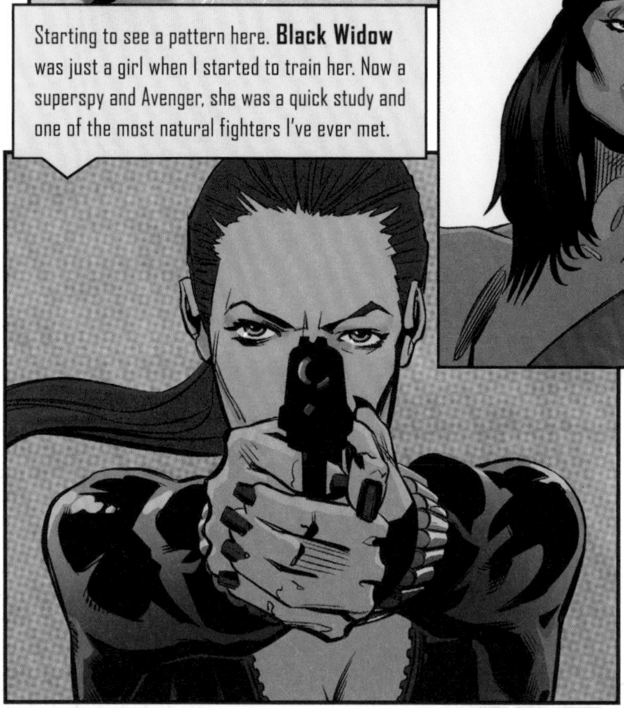
Starting to see a pattern here. **Black Widow** was just a girl when I started to train her. Now a superspy and Avenger, she was a quick study and one of the most natural fighters I've ever met.

Every single one of these women brings something to the mix that I can't, whether it's unwavering discipline, unbridled certainty, or just some misguided optimism. They helped strengthen my weak points, and it goes without saying that I was a better man for just knowing them.

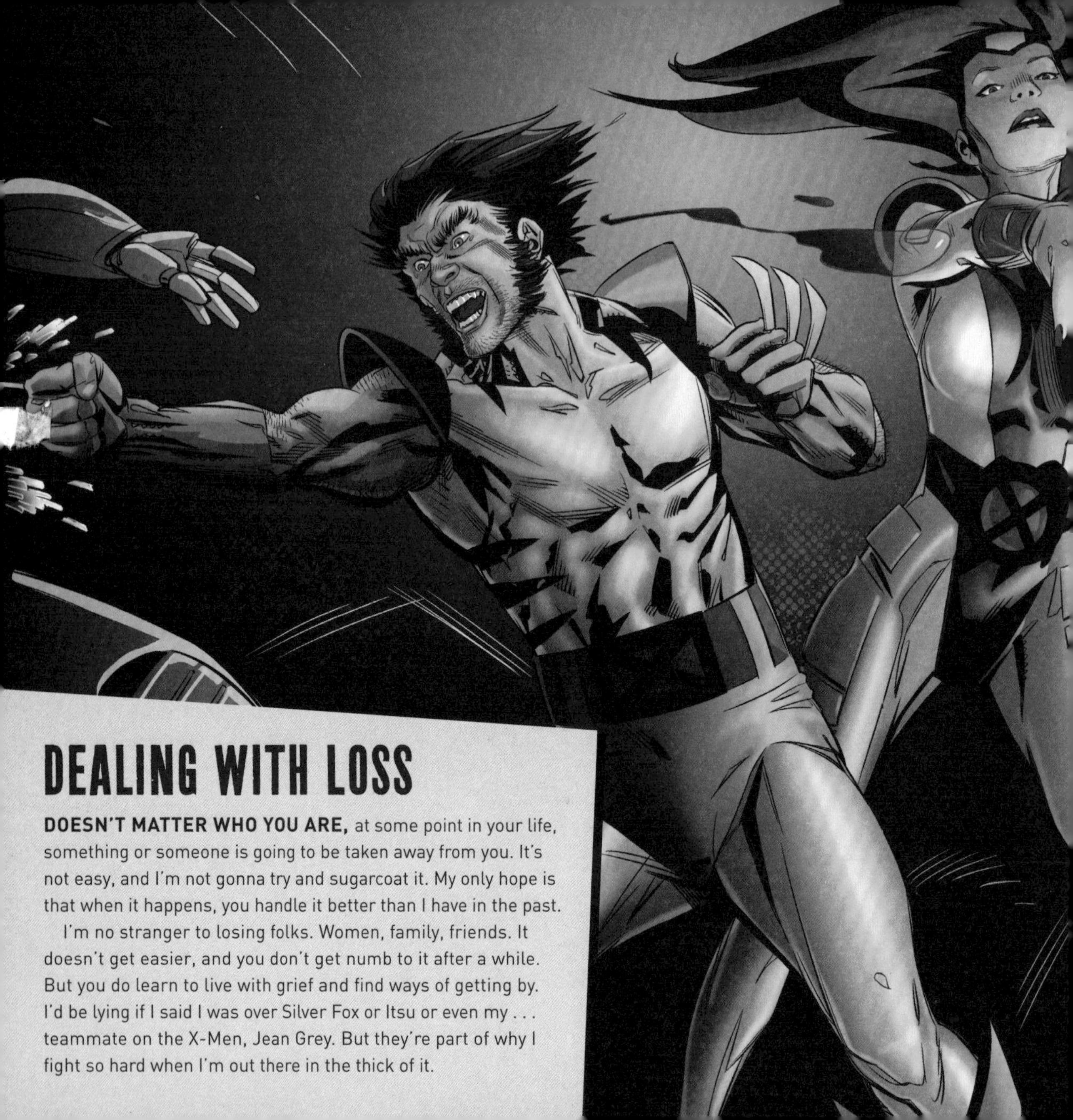

DEALING WITH LOSS

DOESN'T MATTER WHO YOU ARE, at some point in your life, something or someone is going to be taken away from you. It's not easy, and I'm not gonna try and sugarcoat it. My only hope is that when it happens, you handle it better than I have in the past.

I'm no stranger to losing folks. Women, family, friends. It doesn't get easier, and you don't get numb to it after a while. But you do learn to live with grief and find ways of getting by. I'd be lying if I said I was over Silver Fox or Itsu or even my . . . teammate on the X-Men, Jean Grey. But they're part of why I fight so hard when I'm out there in the thick of it.

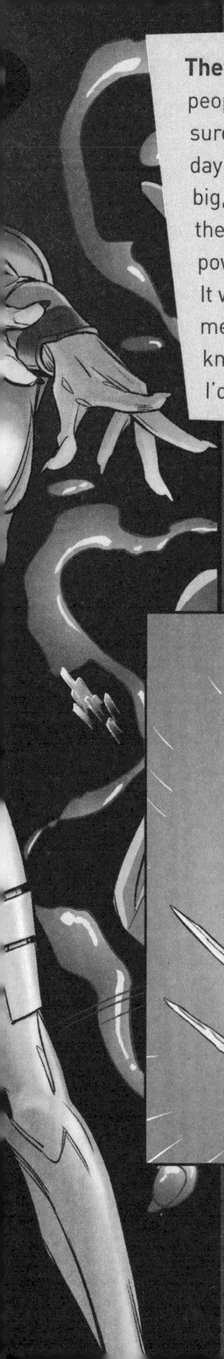

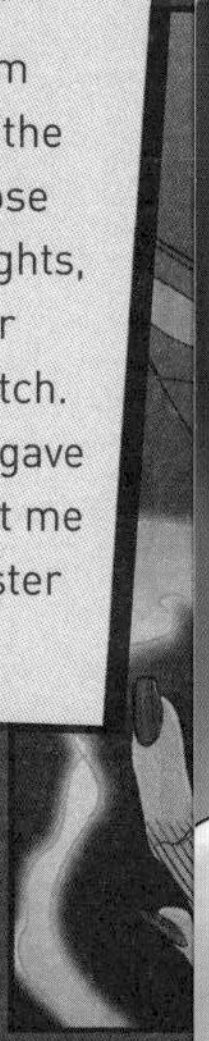

There's another kind of loss for people like us. Loss of powers. I'm sure you all remember "M-day," the day when at the end of one of those big, explosive Super Hero type fights, the majority of mutants lost their powers thanks to the Scarlet Witch. It was that same big battle that gave me back my full memory and let me know exactly what kind of monster I'd been my whole life.

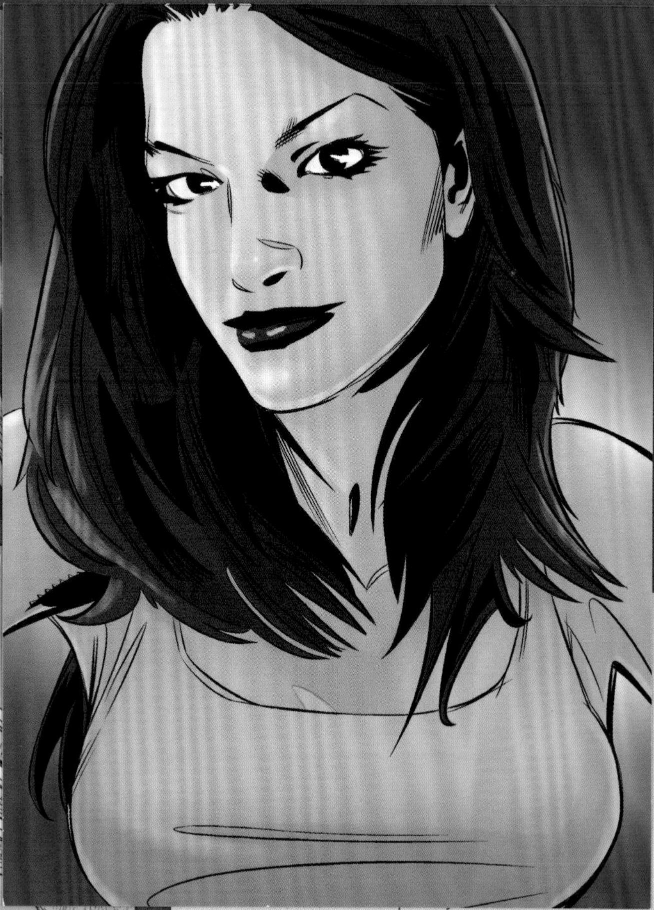

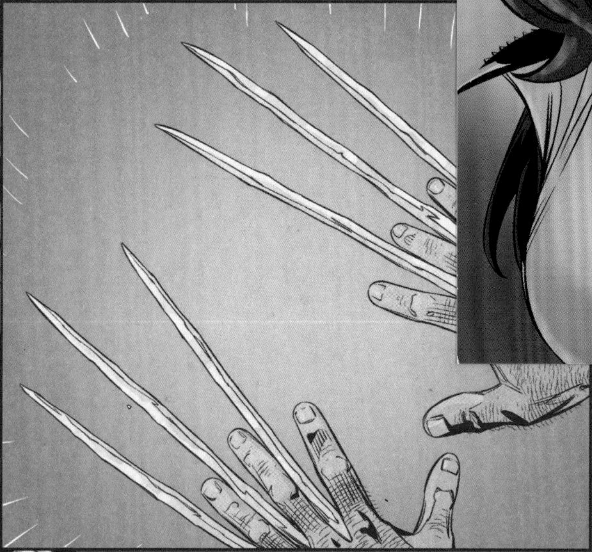

hated their powers, hated who they were. Then "M-Day" comes along, and they can't bear living like the normal folks they spent their whole lives being jealous of.

Loss can mess with your head, and all you can do is keep heading in the direction you were going in before it all hit the fan. Stop and fight back if you need to, but there ain't no point in lingering around a dark place like that for too long.

HOW TO STAY SHARP

FOR ONCE I'M NOT TALKING ABOUT MY CLAWS. Adamantium doesn't really get dull, seeing as how nothing can even scratch the stuff. What I'm talking about is the same song and dance you probably hear in every one of your classes. But you can never hear it too much, and maybe you just need to hear it from me to make it sink in. Your mind is your most important asset in a fight. Anger and grit will only get you so far. You can tune your muscle memory and your mutant powers as much as you want, but it'll all mean nothing if your head's not on straight, and your mind isn't ready for the fight.

Me, I read a lot. Some guys like Sudoku or crosswords and the like, but if it feels like work, I'm probably not going to waste my free time on it. So I read. Mostly stuff that's out of my comfort zone.

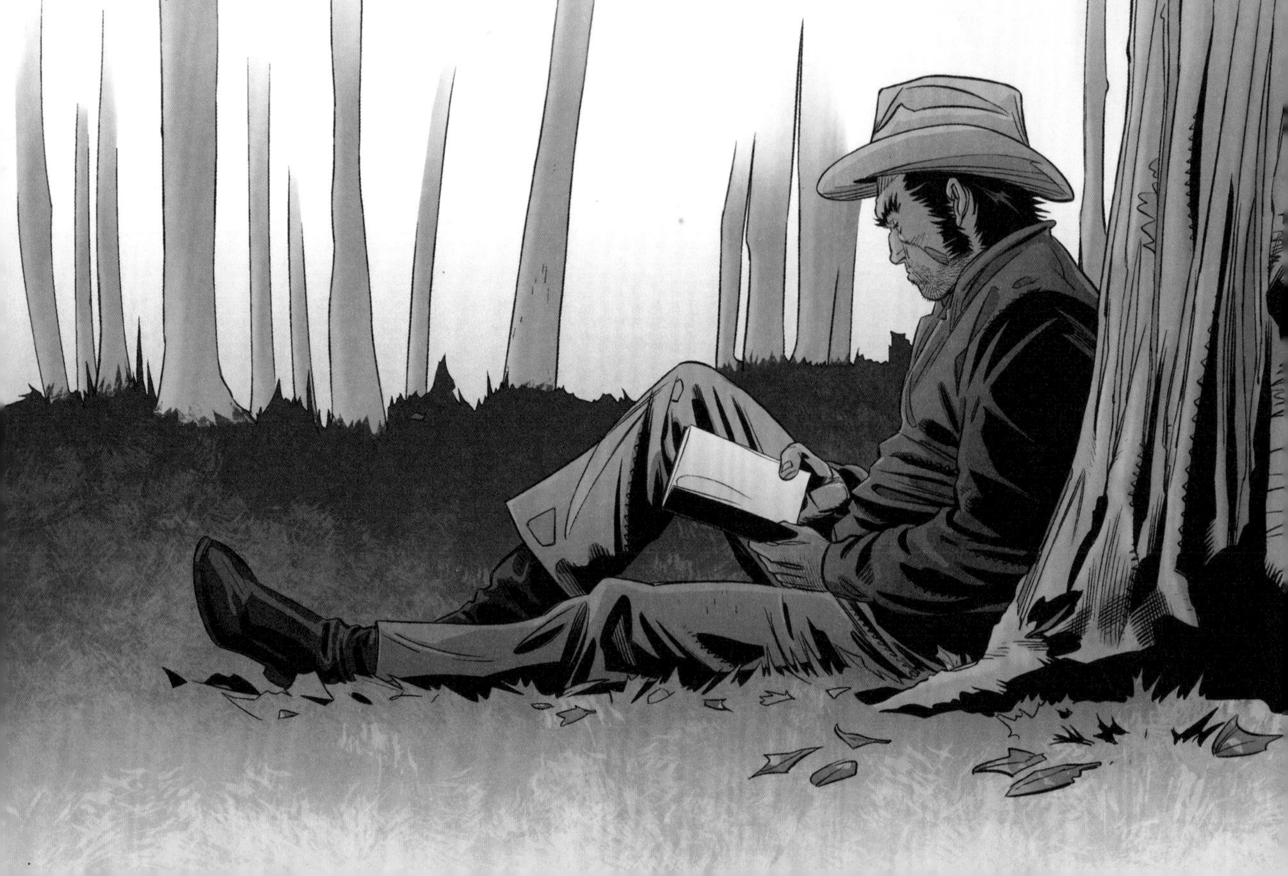

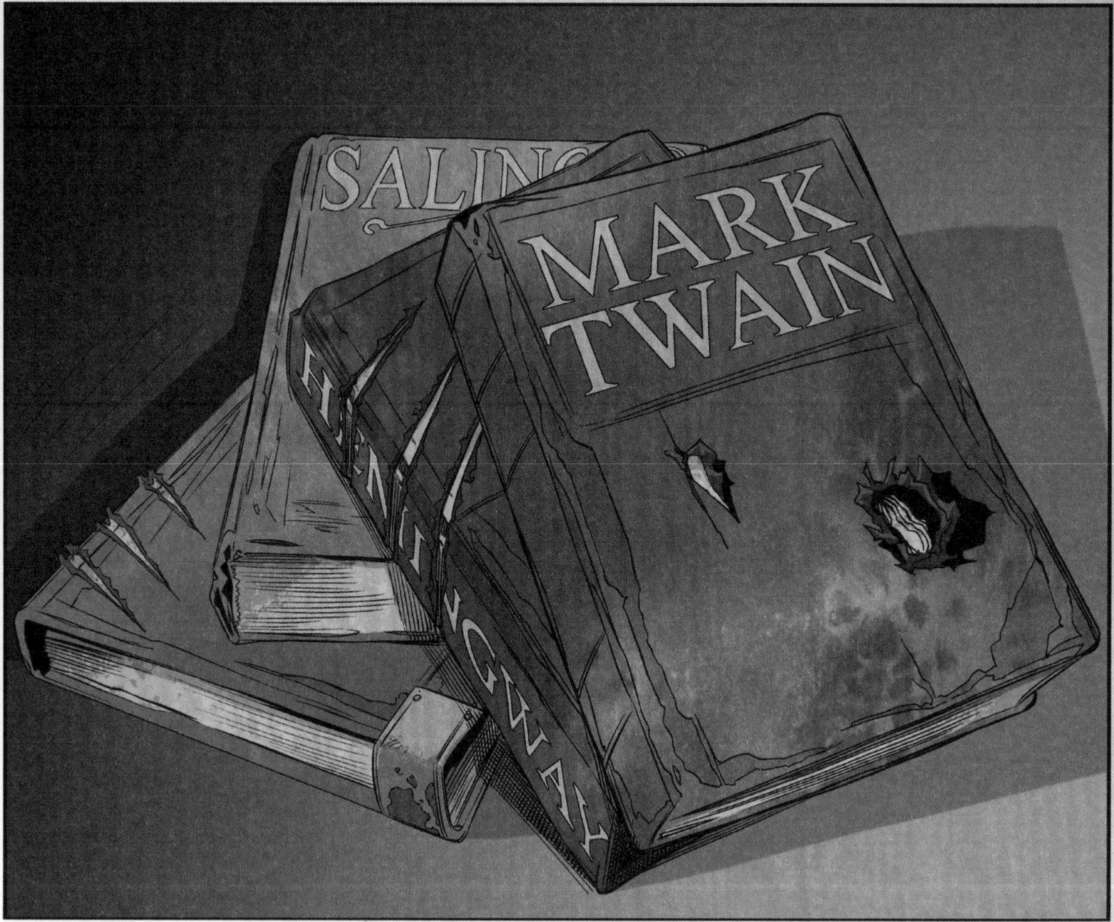
SALING
MARK
TWAIN
HEMINGWAY

Now I'm not gonna give you a reading list, because writers that work for me probably ain't gonna work for you. If it's homework, you're not gonna like it. But read. Everything. Everyone. Thoreau. Whitman. Twain. Faulkner. Poe. Hemingway (used to know the guy personally, by the way). Salinger. Vonnegut. There's a reason these guys are famous. Find out why on your own.

Challenge your head. Your brain's like a muscle. Tear it apart and let it mend itself. And most important, spend some time alone, thinking it all over. You don't mull it over, it's all just words on paper.

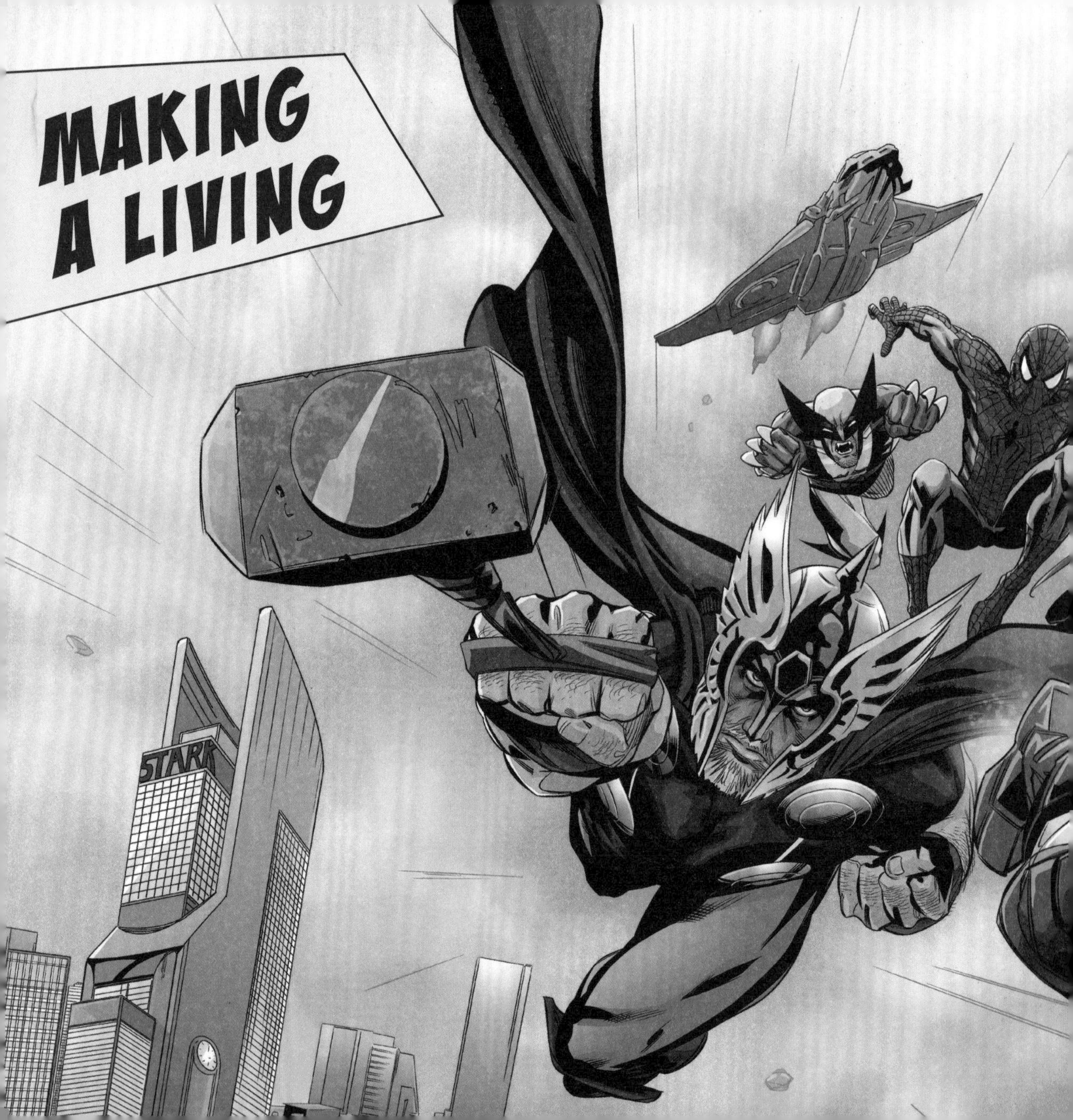
MAKING A LIVING
STARK

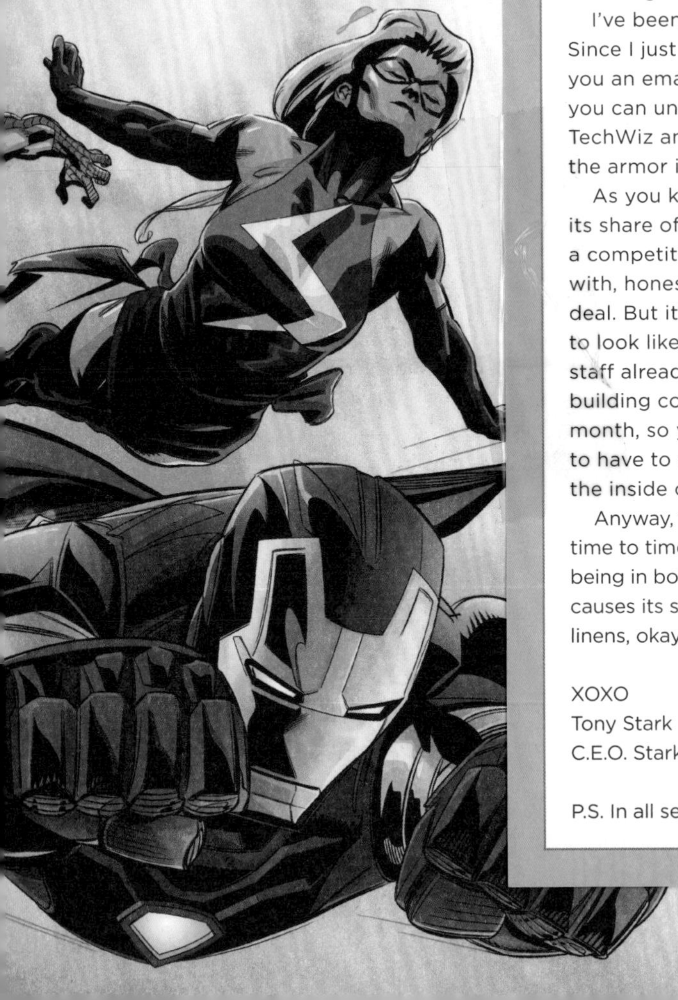

◀ PREVIOUS

REPLY ▼

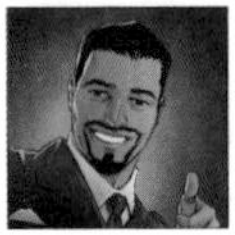

From: Tony Stark [headhoncho@starkindustries.com]
To: Wolverine [logan@starkindustries.com]
11:18 AM (20 minutes ago)

Dear Logan:

I've been talking with Jarvis, and it seems we have an issue. Since I just had my armor polished, I thought it best to shoot you an email rather than bring this up face to face. I'm sure you can understand. I have a photo op in the morning for TechWiz and don't think six puncture holes would show off the armor in the best light.

As you know, being a member of the Avengers comes with its share of perks. The company credit card, catered meals, a competitive salary (not sure who we're even competing with, honestly), and luxury living quarters are all part of the deal. But it's come to my attention that your room is starting to look like something out of the Savage Land. The cleaning staff already has their work cut out for them, what with the building constantly under siege from the Super Villain of the month, so you can see why it might be extra taxing for them to have to deal with a scent that's been described as "what the inside of a bear must smell like."

Anyway, think you could maybe pick up after yourself from time to time? I know you've got a lot on your plate, what with being in both the Avengers and the X-Men, and I'm sure that causes its share of stress. But let's not try to take it out on the linens, okay? Thanks so much.

XOXO
Tony Stark
C.E.O. Stark Industries

P.S. In all seriousness, please don't stab me.

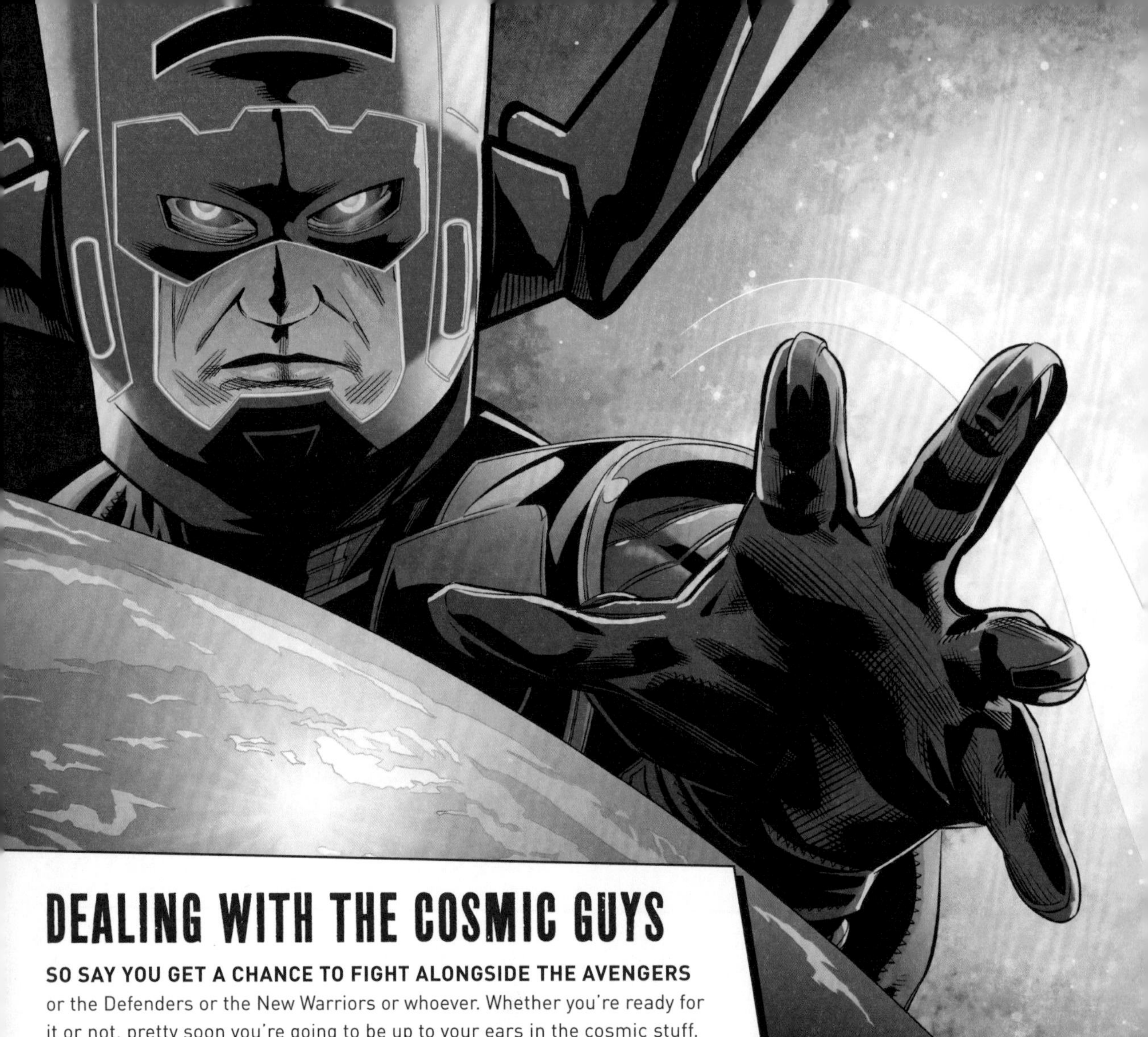

DEALING WITH THE COSMIC GUYS

SO SAY YOU GET A CHANCE TO FIGHT ALONGSIDE THE AVENGERS or the Defenders or the New Warriors or whoever. Whether you're ready for it or not, pretty soon you're going to be up to your ears in the cosmic stuff. Big operatic space wars and single-minded near-omnipotent demigods. Silver guys on surfboards spouting freshman year philosophy. That sort of thing. Most of you are just kids who were born a little different. So you're thinking these big events don't concern you. Join the club.

I'm a guy with claws and unbreakable bones. I'm good in a barroom brawl or a street fight. Can even hold more than my own against most mutants, no matter what their power grade. But you put me in a room with somebody who can control space and time, and I'm about as helpless as an elderly couple in a movie theater full of rowdy teenagers. No matter what I do, there's no way I'm leaving there having enjoyed the experience.

But you can't just lie down and die. You do what you do best, and you take the fight to them as best you can. Even if that means playing the distraction role or fighting the underlings while the Thor-type guys take on the main threat. You're not helping anyone if your ego gets in the way.

And worst-case scenario, you get to be the inspiration. You see the good guys balking even just for a second, and all of a sudden it becomes your job to get their heads back in the fight. If you've got to charge the big bad and sacrifice yourself just to show the heavy hitters how it's done, then you do what you have to do.

I'm pretty sure that no one is comfortable in these kinds of fights. But if the Super Hero road is the one you're taking, comfort isn't in the job description.

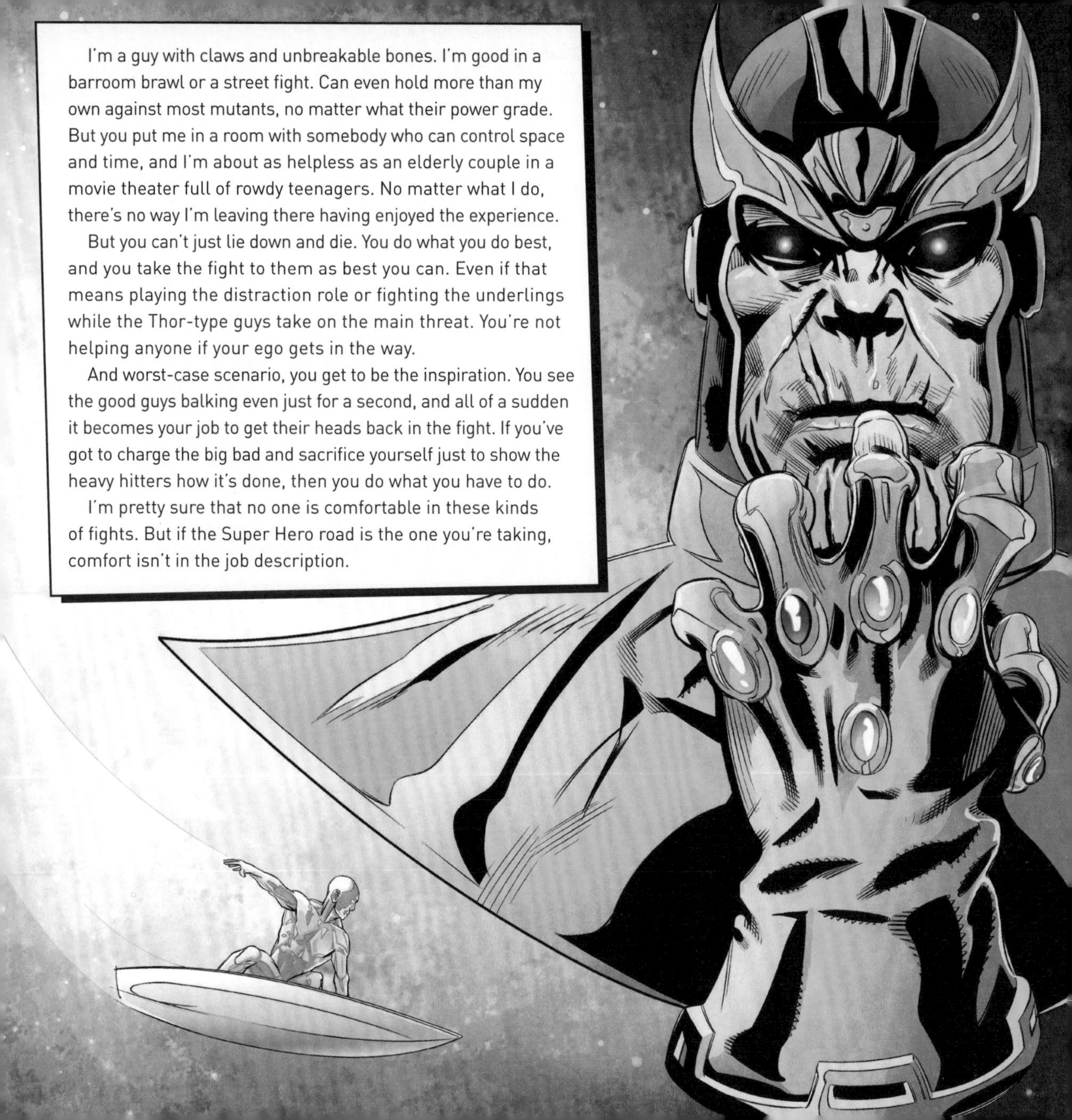

CHOOSING THE WRONG PARTNER

IT SEEMS THAT IN THIS BUSINESS, you don't often have much choice in who you're teamed up with. In my case, I keep finding myself in the company of a certain web-slinger that can't let a minute go by without filling it with mindless chatter. Guy I'm talking about here is Spider-Man. He's an underground icon to some people, a joke to others. I've known for a long time who's under that mask.

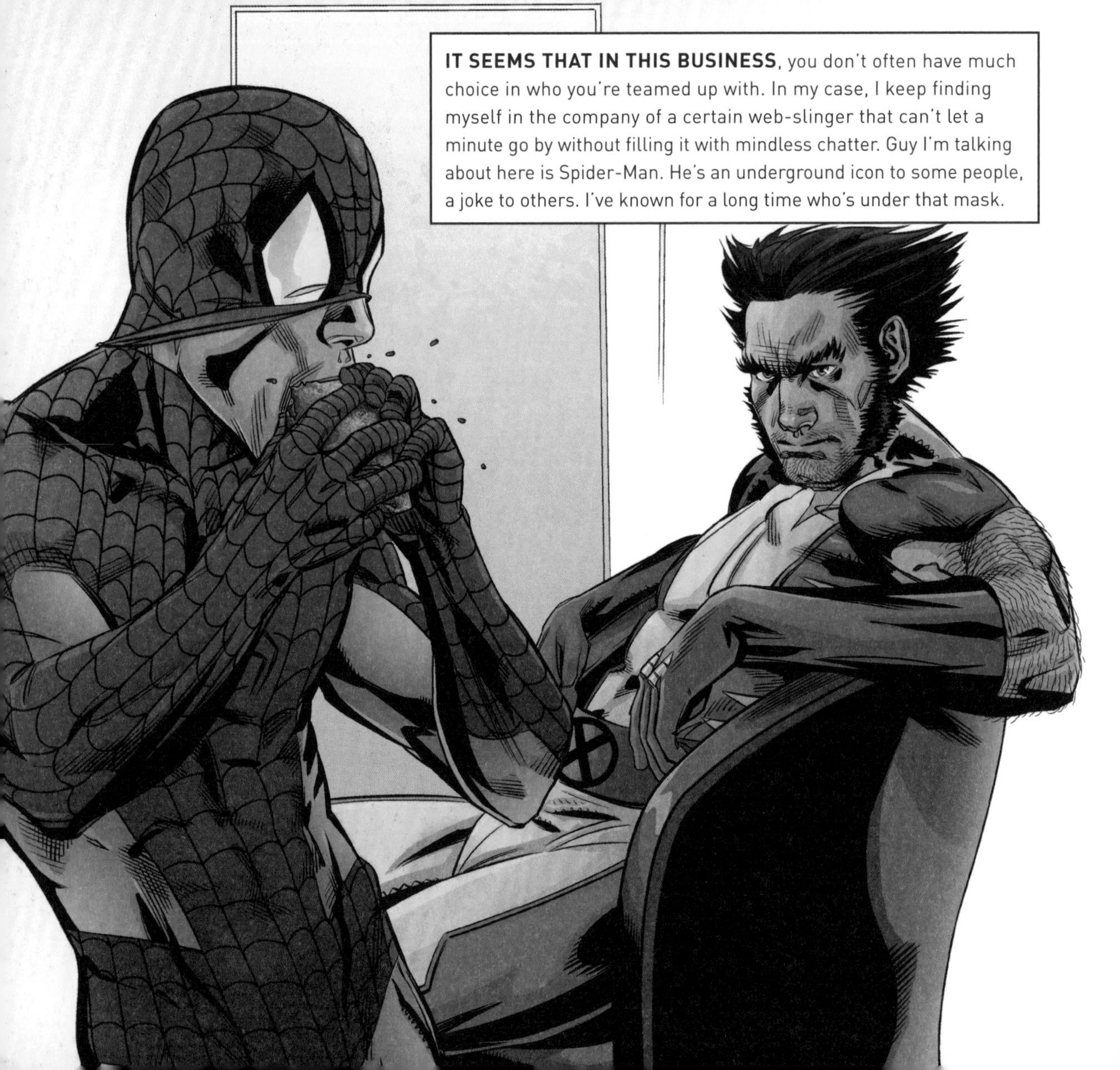

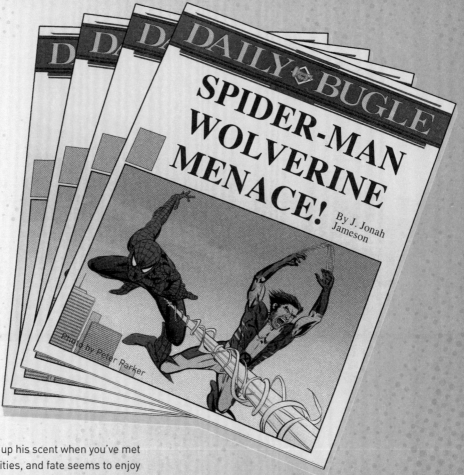

DAILY ◆ BUGLE

SPIDER-MAN WOLVERINE MENACE!

By J. Jonah Jameson

Photo by Peter Parker

Ain't too hard to pick up his scent when you've met him in both his identities, and fate seems to enjoy having us run into each other at the drop of a hat. Kid gets under my skin like nobody's business.

Spider-Man's sharp as a tack and tougher than most any Super Hero you're gonna meet. Problem is, he hides it under a mass of puns and one-liners that pretty much define the term "dad jokes." And he's been telling them since he was a teenager.

So when it came to teaming up with somebody, I can't say that Gabby Twoshoes there was my

first choice. Thing is, we kept finding ourselves as partners and started learning how to work with each other. I've gone on SHIELD missions with this guy, taken on armies of mutants beside him. Heck, we've even been lost in time together. And I can say that I don't think I'd be alive without him.

Point of all this is, when life gives you lemons, you go ahead and use them to beat the hell out of the bad guys.

SO THAT'S IT

I'VE BEEN RAMBLING ON FOR A WHILE NOW, and I think I've about said my piece. I've tried to give you a little idea what it's like being me with the hope you can learn from my mistakes.

This school is an experiment. There's no two ways about it. Every one of you comes here with the hopes of becoming something greater than you are. Finding other people like yourselves. Escaping whatever suburban hell America saddled you with. I don't have any idea if we're gonna do that for you here or if you're gonna slip through the cracks. I'm not Chuck Xavier. I can't know what each of you needs all the time.

You can take what applies to you from this and throw away the rest. Truth is, I'm under a lot of pressure being in charge of a whole generation of mutants. But then again, you've got to live up to my expectations, so I think we're about even.

So go ahead, read this a few more times. Decide what kind of mutant you want to be and get back to me. I got time. One way or another, you're gonna shape the world when you finally walk out of these doors.

Don't let me down, kid.

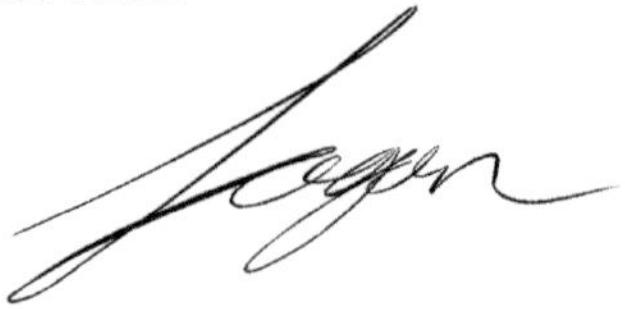

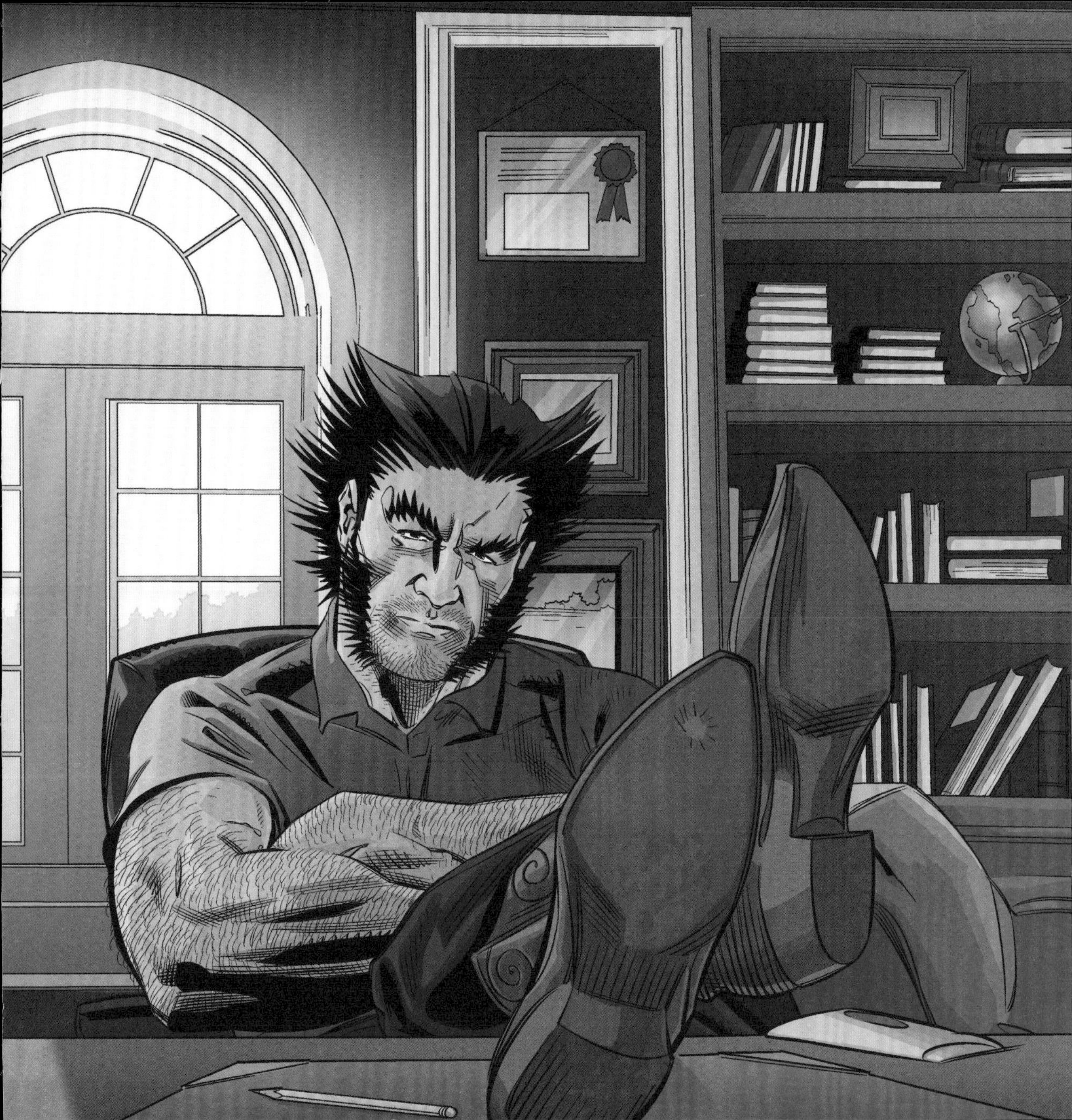

**BANTAM
PRESS**

TRANSWORLD PUBLISHERS
61–63 Uxbridge Road, London W5 5SA
A Random House Group Company
www.transworldbooks.co.uk

marvel.com
© 2014 MARVEL

First published in Great Britain
in 2014 by Bantam Press
an imprint of Transworld Publishers

A CIP catalogue record for this book
is available from the British Library.

ISBN 9780593074244

Addresses for Random House Group Ltd companies outside the
UK can be found at: www.randomhouse.co.uk
The Random House Group Ltd Reg. No. 954009

Published by arrangement with Insight Editions, LP, 10 Paul
Drive, San Rafael, CA 94903, USA

Manufactured in Hong Kong by Insight Editions
10 9 8 7 6 5 4 3 2 1

**ABOUT THE INSIGHT
LEGENDS SERIES**
Insight Legends is a
collectible pop culture
library featuring books
that take an in-depth look
at iconic characters and other elements from
the worlds of comics, movies, and video games.
Packed with special items that give the books an
immersive, interactive feel, the series delivers
unparalleled insight into the best-loved characters
in popular culture and the worlds they inhabit.

**INSIGHT
EDITIONS**

PO Box 3088
San Rafael, CA 94912
www.insighteditions.com

WRITTEN BY Matthew K. Manning
ILLUSTRATED BY Stephen Mooney
INKING BY Stephen Thompson
COLORING BY Lisa Jackson

INSIGHT EDITIONS would like to thank
David Gabriel, Mark Annunziato, Curt Baker,
Tomas Palacios, Jeff Youngquist, Sarah Brunstad,
Brian Overton, Mike Fichera, and Mike O'Sullivan.